Meta Intelligence

Meta Intelligence

Why it Matters More than IQ or EQ

Justice Royal

Acknowledgements

In writing this book, I have drawn on the wisdom of great thinkers throughout history such as Benjamin Franklin, Thomas Edison, and Albert Einstein, as well as contemporary influential people such as Elon Musk, Bill Gates, and Jeff Bezos. You will find their inspiring thoughts sprinkled throughout this book.

Contents

Chapter 1:

Introduction

———

——

—

find it fascinating how as so often happens, it is only when we are faced with adversity that we begin to engage in soul-searching; that we begin to contemplate our thoughts and our actions. And this was indeed the case with me. I was going through life on auto-pilot mode; never once looking within. Like many people, I was just getting by. Then suddenly, I was faced with a series of life challenges that made me examine the poor decisions I had made and the thought processes that led to them.

I began to analyze my mental attitudes and cognitions in an effort to understand and improve them. Before long I developed a new way of thinking which allowed me to make better decisions and achieve more of my goals.

I became interested in thinking in general and began to study and observe how other people thought - especially successful people. I noticed that some people shared my newfound way of thinking, but they were definitely not the majority - most people sleepwalk through life, as I did before my epiphany.

Another observation is that this way of thinking is quite different from either IQ or EQ. These constructs are often regarded as being necessary for success but as I point out in the following two chapters, they have serious limitations.

The people I observed were not all members of Mensa or the Society of Emotional Intelligence. No, the people I observed had varying educational backgrounds as well as varying degrees of emotional intelligence. What they all had in common, though, was an effective way of thinking.

To my surprise, I couldn't find any literature on this type of thinking – everything was either IQ or EQ – which is why I decided to write this book. I call this different way of thinking *Meta Intelligence,* and I refer to the people who think this way as *meta thinkers*. I also affectionately refer to them as the *Meta Intelligentsia*.

Chapter 2:

Why the IQ construct is worse than useless

The big problem with the concept of IQ is that it presumes general intelligence is a fixed entity that is capped by your genes. You are born with either 'smart genes' or 'dumb genes'. You will obtain a certain IQ score and it will remain with you for the rest of your life. This is absolutely absurd, and I can't believe how so many people bought into it. Neuroscientist, Dr. Adrian Owen, isn't convinced of the sanctity of IQ scores either. He had this to say…

"When we looked at the data, the bottom line is the whole concept of IQ – or you having a higher IQ than me – is a myth. There is no such thing as a single measure of IQ or a measure of general intelligence."

-thestar.com/life/2012/12/19

And here is famed Harvard psychologist, Howard Gardner …

"The tasks featured in the IQ test are decidedly microscopic, . . . are remote, in many cases, from everyday life . . . Moreover, the intelligence test reveals little about an individual's potential for further growth."

(Gardner H. , 1983)

It is widely accepted that individuals with high IQs will be more successful than people with low IQs; they will go to better schools and get better jobs etc. Hogwash! The premise of this book is that anyone can improve their thinking and realize their goals regardless of their genetic or demographic makeup. This should be self-evident and perhaps the reason that it isn't lies in the dubious history of IQ tests.

The history of IQ testing is very dark indeed. It is closely intertwined with the history of the eugenics movement.

Eugenicists wanted to improve a population through controlled breeding.

> "By and large, eugenicists thought that (1) intelligence was a unitary psychological trait that could be measured, being quantified as an intelligence quotient (IQ); (2) intelligence was paired with educational achievement, reputation, and economic success; (3) a certain degree of intelligence was necessary to act morally and to foresee the consequences of one's actions. , …, Francis Galton (1922-1911), who coined the term 'eugenics', thought that intelligence was one of the great traits that superior men possessed and contributed most to their success. Reasoning that intelligence was normally distributed within populations and correlated with eminence, he hypothesized in *Hereditary Genius* (1869) that this trait was heritable."

> (Roige, 2014)

Eugenicists typically predicted that whites and the upper class would score higher on IQ tests, and since they developed the tests, their predictions were usually borne out. But as acclaimed anthropologist Stanley Garn points out …

> "If the aborigine drafted an IQ test, all of western civilization would presumably flunk it."

This bias no doubt led to non-whites and the poor being marginalized. It also fueled calls for the segregation and restricted immigration of non-whites. In extreme cases, individuals with low intelligence were forcibly sterilized.

It would appear that eugenicists were more interested in preserving the white upper-class status quo than objectively measuring intelligence and the notion of fixed intelligence suited that agenda perfectly. (Biased) IQ tests would be their tool of choice for demonstrating the intellectual superiority of upper-class whites and the rationale for preserving white upper-class power.

Eugenicists even went so far as to falsify their findings in order to advance their agenda. Sir Cyril Burt was an influential English educational psychologist as well as a member of the British Eugenics Society. He is the father of Britain's notorious 11+ exam which determines which 11-year-olds will attend 'white collar' secondary schools vs 'blue collar' secondary schools. This exam is still in place today.

Burt devoted practically his entire career to trying to prove that Britain's upper class were genetically intellectually superior to its lower classes, and in 1946, he was knighted for his efforts. Sir Burt studied twins separated at birth and 'found' that they had virtually identical IQ scores. Fortunately, Princeton psychologist, Leon J. Kamin noticed Burt's 'too good to be true' numbers and exposed him as a fraud in his important work, *The Science and Politics of I.Q.* (Kamin, 1974), which discredited the work of eugenicists like Burt and dealt a serious blow to the eugenics movement. Nonetheless, modern day eugenicists still attempt to exonerate Burt.

The concept of intelligence as malleable, as something anyone can improve and grow, did not fit well with eugenic plans. Yet as anyone who has continuously improved their thought process can tell you, this dynamic component of intelligence is extremely powerful.

> *"One is not born a genius;*
> *one becomes a genius."*
>
> -Simone de Beauvoir

CHAPTER 3:

WHY EQ IS NOT ENOUGH

ntelligence as measured by IQ tests was always thought to be the most important factor in an individual's success. However, studies showed that this is in fact not the case: e.g. it was found that people with the highest levels of IQ outperform those with average IQs 20% of the time, while people with average IQs outperform those with high IQs 70% of the time (Bradberry & Greaves, 2009). As a result of these findings, researchers searched for another variable that would better predict success.

The new messianic variable was Emotional Intelligence (EQ). EQ is the awareness and management of one's emotions as well as that of others. EQ was found to correlate better with success than IQ, and so it quickly worked its way into popular culture. Once people realized that IQ didn't correlate highly with success, they jumped onto the EQ bandwagon trampling on cognitive intelligence in the process. The pendulum had now swung too far in the opposite direction. Suddenly, it was all about emotions; cognitive intelligence didn't matter anymore. This is also ridiculous. You *do* need cognitive intelligence to be successful. In fact, I would argue that cognitive intelligence is *the* most important factor for success – just not the kind of cognitive intelligence that is associated with IQ tests.

You can't just 'feel' your way to success. The fact that EQ has limitations is borne out both experimentally and anecdotally. One surprising finding of EQ studies was that CEOs scored low on EQ tests (Bradberry & Greaves, 2009). More recently, Bradberry found that …

"For the titles of director and above, scores descend faster than a snowboarder on a black diamond. CEOs, on average, have the lowest EQ scores in the workplace."

(Bradberry, 2015)

Anecdotally, it has been an open secret that some of the greatest business leaders such as Steve Jobs were very low in EQ (Dalio, 2017).

So, if it's not IQ or EQ, then what is the most important variable for success? Well, I would posit that it is meta intelligence which I will delineate in the remainder of this book.

Chapter 4:

So, what is meta intelligence anyway?

———

——

—

"To change your world, begin by changing yourself.
To change yourself, begin by changing your point of view"

-Wu Hsin

The Cognitive Complement to EQ

———

—

One way of thinking about meta intelligence is that it is the natural cognitive complement to EQ (and like EQ, I will use an abbreviation, *MQ*, to refer to either meta intelligence or meta intelligence quotient). EQ & MQ are the yin and yang of the self awareness universe. Where one is concerned with emotions, the other is concerned with cognitive processes.

So, if EQ can be defined as the awareness and management of one's *emotions* and that of others, meta intelligence can be defined as the awareness and management of one's *cognitive processes* and that of others. Emotionally intelligent people are preoccupied with how they and others feel. Meta intelligent people pay more attention to how they and others think. It is important to note that the two constructs are not mutually exclusive – one can be both emotionally intelligent as well as meta intelligent.

A more extensive definition of meta intelligence is the ability to

…

1. Recognize and understand our own cognitive processes.
2. Recognize and understand the cognitive processes of others.
3. Discern between different cognitive processes and label them appropriately.
4. Effectively manage our own cognitive processes.
5. Effectively manage the cognitive processes of others.
6. Use cognitive information to guide thinking.
7. Use cognitive information to guide behavior.
8. Use cognitive information to judiciously handle interpersonal relationships.
9. Manage and/or adjust cognitive processes to adapt to environments.
10. Manage and/or adjust cognitive processes to achieve one's goal(s).
11. Reflect on cognitive processes to improve one's learning ability.
12. Reflect on cognitive processes to improve one's thinking ability.

I will refer to these meta intelligent abilities throughout this book. They are all important and worthwhile abilities to have, but it is perhaps the last which is most noteworthy because it flies in the face of conventional wisdom. Our thinking ability is not static – it can be improved by thinking meta intelligently. We can in effect make ourselves smarter by thinking smarter!

MQ concerns itself with cognitive self-awareness (thinking about one's thinking and cognitive abilities, and how to improve them), which is why I call it *meta* intelligence. But MQ is much more than just self-contemplation or critical thinking, and while it is partly those things, it is not navel gazing, philosophizing, or new age woo-woo; it is a proactive, practical, and goal directed approach to managing one's thinking and actions in an ever-changing and complex world.

Furthermore, while EQ is associated with emotional empathy, MQ is associated with cognitive empathy. Like EQ, MQ recognizes that no individual is an island – we are all parts of an interconnected social system where we impact others and others most definitely impact us. Therefore, it makes sense that we should understand how other people think as well as the reasons for their actions.

And most importantly, like EQ and unlike IQ, MQ is an ability that can be improved with conscious effort and practice.

*"Knowing others is intelligence.
Knowing yourself is true wisdom.
Mastering others is strength.
Mastering yourself is true power."*

-Lao Tzu

AN EMPOWERING MINDSET

———

—

"Once your mindset changes, everything on the
outside will change along with it."

-Steve Maraboli

MQ can also be thought of as a mindset, but it is much more powerful than a regular positive or growth mindset because it is more proactive, systematic, and focused.

Meta intelligent individuals know that by systematically identifying and managing their cognitive processes, they will rapidly improve their thinking and grow intellectually.

Besides optimally managing one's thinking processes, MQ aims to optimally manage one's attitudes. MQ individuals continuously monitor their beliefs and attitudes and replace any disempowering beliefs or attitudes with empowering ones (I will discuss the meta intelligent attitudes that are conducive with intellectual growth in a later chapter).

Thus, in these respects, MQ can be regarded as a dynamic and empowering mindset.

17

"Change your thoughts and you change your world"

-Norman Vincent Peale

A HIGHER LEVEL OF THINKING

———

—

I will discuss cognitive processes that MQ monitors throughout this book. An example of such cognitive processes is provided to us by Benjamin Bloom. Benjamin Bloom was an educational psychologist who formulated a hierarchical classification of cognitive processes in 1956. His taxonomy was later revised by (Anderson, Krathwohl, & others, 2001) and includes six distinct cognitive processes from remembering (lowest order) to creating (highest order)…

1. Remembering: find or remember information
2. Understanding: make sense of information
3. Applying: use information in a new situation
4. Analyzing: take information apart and explore relationships
5. Evaluating: critically examine information and make judgements
6. Creating: use information to create something new

The first three processes are regarded as lower order processes and the last three are regarded as higher order processes. Bloom aimed to promote higher levels of thinking in education. He was a visionary who realized that the educational system of the day would not be able to turn out graduates who had the thinking skills necessary for the workplaces of the future. Students were being taught simple rote learning and thinking (the lower order processes) but they would require higher order processes (analysis, evaluation, creation) for the coming knowledge economy. Higher order thinking skills (HOTS) such as problem solving, decision making, & critical thinking are built on these higher order processes.

Many people still only use lower order thinking skills while others use higher order thinking skills only some of the time. Meta thinkers on the other hand focus a lot of their mental energy on the higher three processes. Meta thinkers are constantly analyzing, evaluating, & improving their cognition as well as everything else in their lives. The meta intelligentsia are also driven to create. They create products and services, not just use them. So, don't be content to just read; give writing a try. Don't just appreciate art; create it as well.

=-=-=

Bloom's taxonomy was adequate for the first part of the 21st century and the third industrial revolution, but the rapid evolution of information and other technologies has left many feeling overwhelmed and anxious. Innovations in technology have impacted every facet of society – from the way we interact and communicate to the way we buy and pay for goods. It seems we do just about everything electronically and through the world wide web – we have become *techno-centric* societies.

Together with the expanding role of technology, we have also become *info-centric* societies. Information plays a central role in society today and because of the internet and ubiquitous mobile communication devices, the amount of information available to everyone is unprecedented.

And we are now on the cusp of the fourth industrial revolution, which is characterized by advanced artificial intelligence and robotics. Third revolution automation decimated blue collar jobs; fourth revolution automation threatens to do the same for white collar jobs. Everyone will be at risk except the meta intelligent who can create things robots can't.

Moreover, as society grows and becomes more complex, so to, do its problems. The solutions required to solve complex problems such as effective resource allocation and ecological disruption will require a different mindset and *mindware*. Traditional ways of thinking will no longer suffice to meet this challenge. It will require innovative thinking on a level that only MQ can provide.

> *"You can't solve problems with the same kind of*
> *thinking that created them.*
> *A new type of thinking is essential if mankind is to*
> *survive and move toward higher levels."*
>
> -Albert Einstein

To meet the challenges of today's rapidly evolving and complex society, MQ employs SMARTER thinking that is…

- **S**ystems-minded
- **M**etacognitive
- **A**daptive
- **R**esourceful
- **T**ask-conscious
- **E**volving
- **R**ational

I describe SMARTER thinking in the next chapter.

Chapter 5:

A Smarter

Way of Thinking

———

——

—

The aim of MQ is to enable you to consciously manage how you think, so that you think more effectively. Meta intelligent individuals employ SMARTER thinking to do just that.

To reiterate, SMARTER thinking is **s**ystems-minded, **m**etacognitive, **a**daptive, **r**esourceful, **t**ask-conscious, **e**volving, & **r**ational.

SYSTEMS-MINDED THINKING

———

—

This is otherwise known as systems thinking and is not to be confused with systematic thinking. According to acclaimed systems theorist, Peter Senge of the *New England Complex Systems Institute*,

"Systems thinking is a discipline for seeing wholes. It is a framework for seeing interrelationships rather than things, for seeing 'patterns of change' rather than static snapshots.

...

The essence of mastering systems thinking lies in seeing patterns where others see only events and forces to react to. Yet few are trained to see dynamic complexity.

...

Most of the problems faced by humankind concern our inability to grasp and manage the increasingly complex systems of our world."

-Peter Senge (Senge, 2010)

Successful people think in terms of systems. They are able to see the overall structure of things while the average person can just see individual pieces. Bill Gates, for example, when looking at a problem, asks questions such as: "What are the different factors involved in this problem?" and "How does the system work as a whole?".

Meta intelligent people understand that living beings, societies, and ecosystems in general are complex systems with many interconnected and interdependent parts and subsystems. Consequently, in studying complex systems, it is not enough to break the system down and study the components separately as you would with analytical thinking. That is because the components act differently when separated from the system. As part of a system, they interact with other components, and it is those interactions that must be studied as well.

Having many interacting components results in a large number of cause and effect relationships, and a component may trigger a cause and effect chain reaction resulting in the initial cause being distant in space and time from the ultimate effect. This means that complex systems may have complex problems which require more sophisticated problem-solving approaches such as examining root causes. It also becomes important to avoid complex problems by employing preemptive techniques such as second order thinking.

Jeff Bezos, the CEO of Amazon, is a meta intelligent SMARTER thinker who also happens to be the richest person on earth. He frequently talks about the importance of understanding root causes and second order consequences.

Root Cause Analysis (RCA)

RCA aims to fix a problem at the root, not at the surface. If you do not fix a problem at the root, it will just resurface again like an unwanted stubborn weed. Two useful techniques that can be used in RCA are the W5 and 5why techniques. These are excellent techniques to gain a deeper understanding of any issue. W5 asks the journalist's questions such as what, when, where, who, why, & how it happened. 5why starts off by asking why and then keeps asking *why* to every response until the real reason reveals itself.

Second Order Thinking

This is thinking beyond the first consequence of an action. People tend to see only the first consequence of their actions. They don't realize that the first consequence may cause a secondary effect which may in turn cause a tertiary effect and so on down the line. Most people, it seems, undertake actions that are first order positive and avoid actions that are first order negative. They do not look beyond the initial action. Unfortunately for them, an initial positive effect is often followed by subsequent negative effects (and vice versa).

METACOGNITIVE THINKING

———

—

Metacognitive thinking is thinking about your cognitive processes and trying to optimize them, especially as it relates to higher order thinking skills. Many people, it would seem, do not appreciate the true power of metacognitive thinking and they go through life on auto-pilot mode letting others do their thinking for them. Metacognitive thinking is crucial for self-direction and personal growth and it is also an important skill for learning and problem-solving in the 21st century.

Working in the knowledge economy means knowing what knowledge you know and don't know, as well as what knowledge you should learn (accurate and valuable) and shouldn't learn (not accurate or not valuable). Metacognitive thinkers are always evaluating what knowledge and skills they need to learn to be effective. They also know that they need to be autodidactic or self-learners, and they constantly evaluate and improve their learning strategies.

"Identify and learn valuable knowledge at the right time. The value of knowledge isn't static."

-Michael Simmons

In a similar vein, solving complex problems requires finding effective strategies to solve them. Metacognitive thinkers are always monitoring, evaluating, and optimizing their strategies. If certain strategies are not leading to their goals, they modify them or develop new strategies.

ADAPTIVE THINKING

———

—

"The mind adapts and converts to its own purposes the obstacle to our acting. The impediment to action advances action. What stands in the way becomes the way."

-Marcus Aurelius

Adaptive thinking is the ability to quickly and effectively adjust your thoughts and behavior in response to a change in your environment (e.g. new information, technology, events, obstacles). Societies and life in general are not only complex, they are also highly dynamic. And this has never been truer than in the 21st century. Success in the 21st century will go to those who can deal quickly and effectively with change.

Where metacognition involved an awareness of the self, adaptive thinking entails an acute awareness of others and one's environment. It also entails the ability to be flexible and alter your stance or way of doing things if changing circumstances warrant it. People with non-adaptive or rigid thinking continue doing the same things despite changing conditions. They do not change course when an iceberg is approaching.

> *"I can't change the direction of the wind, but I can adjust my sails so that I always reach my destination."*
>
> -Jimmy Dean

Situational Awareness

One important component of adaptive thinking is situational awareness (SA).

There are various informal definitions of SA such as being aware of your immediate surroundings so that you are better able to respond to imminent threats. This is typically how most people think of SA, but SA can have wider scope than that e.g. being aware of your environment so that you are better able to respond to changes. Changes may include threats, anomalies, as well as opportunities.

A more formal definition was provided by psychologist Mica Endsley which splits SA into 3 phases: Perception, Comprehension, & Projection. (Endsley, 1995)

1. Perception of the relevant data & elements in an environment. Includes detection of an event that deviates

from the norm. (Inputting information. Picking up cues from the environment. Collecting raw data.)

2. Comprehension of the meaning & significance of the current situation. (Processing information. Putting those cues together to holistically understand what is going on. Analyzing, synthesizing, & evaluating the data.)

3. Projection of the future status of the situation. (Providing a spatial-temporal projection of future states and events. Using that understanding to predict what may happen next. Using statistical & forecasting models.)

Military theorists since Sun Tzu have considered situational awareness to be particularly important in battle. Consider the following scenario as a simple example of the SA process:

1. *Detecting* of enemy troop movements – amassing along the border.

2. *Understanding* that large numbers of enemy troops on the border constitute a serious threat.

3. *Predicting* that the enemy is likely to invade.

The military planner can then decide what course of action to take.

Situational awareness also figures prominently in aviation where many crashes can be attributed to a breakdown in the pilot's SA. This was undoubtedly the case in the tragic crash that claimed the life of NBA legend Kobe Bryant. The pilot of the helicopter noticed the fog, but he either underestimated the threat it posed, or he overestimated his ability to deal with it. This led to the fatal decision not to abort the flight and to continue flying to the destination.

Resourceful Thinking

———

—

A society that is increasingly complex and dynamic requires one to be increasingly resourceful to meet its challenges. Being resourceful means having the ability to find quick and clever ways to solve problems or achieve one's goals. One of the best ways to do this is to have. a large selection of cognitive tools at one's disposal. Resourceful thinkers are always looking to expand their cognitive toolbox. They 'borrow' 'power tools' from other enlightened thinkers and they also create their own.

One such set of power tools are *mental models*. Mental models are concepts or internal representations of how the world works. They help you solve problems and make decisions, as well as provide an accurate lens with which to view the world. You can also think of mental models as apps for the mind, and they constitute an integral part of one's *mindware*. Mindware refers to the mental knowledge and procedures that a person uses to solve problems or make decisions.

Mindware is something you continuously update and acquire over a lifetime and in today's world it is much more important than native intelligence. Developing and expanding one's mindware is an important preoccupation of meta intelligent people. Effective mindware together with an empowering mindset form the foundation of meta intelligence.

In my study of successful people, I noticed that they think in terms of mental models more so than the average person. For example, I talked about Bill Gates and *systems thinking* and how Jeff Bezos often uses the *root cause* and *second order thinking* mental models.

Another mental model Bezos is famous for using is his *regret minimization framework* for decision-making. Regret minimization involves projecting yourself into the future and looking back on a decision you must make today. You choose the option you will regret the least, e.g. if you decide to maintain the status quo and not take a risk but you seriously regret it in your projected future, then go ahead and take that risk. This is the model he used when he decided to quit his job and go all-in on Amazon.

=-=-=

It is Charlie Munger, however, who can probably be most credited with bringing the concept of mental models to the mainstream. Charlie Munger is Warren Buffett's right-hand man at Berkshire Hathaway and in a speech in 1995 (*The Psychology of Human Misjudgement*), he talked about mental models…

"What is elementary, worldly wisdom? Well, the first rule is that you can't really know anything if you just remember isolated facts and try and bang 'em back. If the facts don't hang together on a latticework of theory, you don't have them in a usable form. You've got to have models in your head. And you've got to array your exper ence — both vicarious and direct — on this latticework of models. You may have noticed students who just try to remember and pound back what is remembered. Well, they fail in school and in life. You've got to hang experience on a latticework of models in your head."

One of Charlie's favourite mental models is *inversion*: envisioning the opposite of what you want to achieve so you can avoid the path that gets you there. In the following famous quote, Munger inverts success…

"Invert! Always invert! Turn a situation or problem upside down. Look at it backward. What happens if all our plans go wrong? Where don't we want to go, and how do you get there? Instead of looking for success, make a list of how to fail instead – through sloth, envy, resentment, self-pity, entitlement, all the mental habits of self-defeat. Avoid these qualities and you will succeed. Tell me where I'm going to die so I don't go there."

-Charlie Munger

Munger and Warren Buffett are known for creating and making good use of mental models to build their Berkshire Hathaway empire. One of Buffett's mental models is the *circle of competence*: know what you're good at and focus within that circle and know where this circle's boundaries meet your areas of incompetence.

Other notable proponents of mental models include …

- Richard Feynman - the *Feynman technique*: understanding a concept by explaining it to a 5th grader [through *recursive simplification*]
- Daniel Kahneman – *cognitive biases* (I will discuss biases in the skills chapter and throughout this book)
- Elon Musk – *first order principles* (I will discuss this model in the resources chapter)

In the meantime, if you want to learn more about mental models, you can follow Shane Parrish's *Farnam Street* blog, fs.blog. The name is taken from the street address of Berkshire

Hathaway. Farnam Street is devoted to helping us better understand the world through mental models.

37

Task-conscious thinking

———

—

While formulating the concept of meta intelligence, I observed how people thought and I noticed that some individuals paid more attention to their tasks than others. There was one type of individual who was rather different from the rest. This type of individual was obsessed with how they did things. No matter how large or how small the task, they would always try to determine the best way of doing it.

I call it task-conscious thinking as opposed to task-oriented thinking because it's about more than just crossing things off as you complete them – it's being mindful of the process and evaluating the actions you take, e.g. their utility, effectiveness, efficiency, etc. Task-conscious individuals are always paying attention to what's working and not working and adjusting accordingly. Thus task-consciousness can be viewed as metacognitive thinking applied to tasks or processes.

I don't think anybody demonstrates this type of thinking better than Elon Musk. Here are some of his musings …

I think it's important to have a feedback loop, where you're constantly thinking about what you've done and how you could be doing it better.

Constantly think about how you could be doing things better and quest oning yourself.

Don't delude yourself into thinking something's working when it's not, or you're gonna get fixated on a bad solution.

Don't waste time on stuff that doesn't actually make things better.

Tony Robbins is another meta intelligent individual who demonstrates task-consciousness. He frequently stresses the importance of taking action and then monitoring the action you've taken …

The path to success is to take massive determined action.

[And then …]

Learning from what doesn't work, changing your approach until you get to where you want is really what makes someone succeed long term in any context.

Tim Ferriss is also highly task-conscious. His book, *The 4 Hour Workweek,* is a manual on how to design your ideal lifestyle by optimally managing your tasks …

There are two synergistic approaches for increasing productivity that are inversions of each other:

1. Limit tasks to the important to shorten work time (Pareto's 80/20 Principle).
2. Shorten work time to limit tasks to the important (Parkinson's Law).

*

Success is a result of completing the *important* tasks

*

EVOLVING THINKING

———

—

Evolve: to change or develop slowly, often into a better, more complex, or more advanced state.

-Webster's dictionary

The notion that one's thinking can evolve is completely foreign to many people. Meta intelligent people, on the other hand, are always actively improving their thinking.

They know that their thinking must evolve because everything around them is evolving. They are perpetually self-learning and updating their mindset and mindware based on feedback they receive.

If their beliefs and assumptions no longer mesh with the outside world, they will improve them.

If their mental models no longer accurately represent the real world, they will improve them.

If their problem-solving methods prove inadequate, they will improve them.

And so forth.

Failure to evolve our thinking will result in it becoming obsolete and by extension we then become obsolete. We need a minimum level of evolution just to stay relevant. We need constant intellectual evolution if we are to succeed.

RATIONAL THINKING

———

—

Rationality is typically divided into two parts: rationality of one's beliefs (epistemic rationality) and rationality of one's behaviors (instrumental rationality). Rational beliefs are those that are representative of reality. Rational behaviors are those that move you in the direction of your goals.

Meta intelligent individuals regularly check their beliefs and behaviors to make sure they are both accurate and useful.

Being rational doesn't seem too difficult, but it is. The reason for this is that we are not machines. We are emotional entities replete with emotional biases and prejudices which adversely affect our decision-making capabilities.

We also suffer from cognitive load and information processing limitations and as a result our minds employ numerous mental short-cuts (heuristics) which do not always lead to optimal results. When these mental short-cuts form a regular pattern of thinking, they are known as cognitive biases.

Meta intelligent people recognize and manage their biases so that they can make better decisions.

=-=-=

Even if we were not always rational, it was still assumed that rationality went hand in hand with intelligence, i.e. intelligent individuals were deemed more rational than less intelligent ones. However, cognitive scientist, Keith Stanovich debunked this assumption. He studied the relationship between intelligence and rationality and scientifically determined what many of us already suspected: smart people frequently do dumb things! He called this condition, *dysrationalia*. (Stanovich, 2015)

Author, Jon Moore, sums it up well...

"People always confuse intelligence with rational thinking and skepticism. I think it's a big mistake to assume anyone that follows a cult, religion, political party we don't like, etc. is 'stupid.' But it's fair to say that if you follow something irrational, you are acting irrationally (at least as it pertains to that one specific act.) People can be smart - even brilliant - without necessarily being rational. Sometimes it's easy for people to be skeptical to most things, but with one or two glaring blind spots. If you don't spend a good portion of time playing devil's advocate with your own dearly held beliefs, odds are that there will be at least a couple of them that are irrational, even if you're one of the smartest people around."

-Jon Moore

Crafty propagandists and marketers have long considered the masses to be largely irrational and easily bamboozled and manipulated through sophistry and emotional appeals. Before Liane Moriarty became a best-selling author, she worked in the advertising industry and had this to say about it:

"One of the jobs of advertising was to give the consumer rational reasons for their irrational purchases."

"There's a sucker born every minute."

- P. T. Barnum

The best way to avoid being a sucker is to develop SMARTER thinking skills!

CHAPTER 6:

MASTERING COGNITIVE SELF-AWARENESS

———

——

—

"Knowing yourself is the beginning of all wisdom"

-Aristotle

"An unexamined life is not worth living."
"To find yourself think for yourself."

-Socrates

elf-awareness is God's gift to mankind, yet most of us never use it to its fullest potential. It is only by reflecting on our thoughts that we can consciously shape and guide them. This allows us to be in control of our own minds. When you are in control, you can improve yourself and accomplish great things. Bad things tend to happen when you are not in control, e.g. your primitive brain might take control of your mind as in an amygdala hijack, or your mind might get hijacked by other people, or your thoughts might just run around your mind willy-nilly, with no rhyme or reason.

"No man is free who is not master of himself."

-Epictetus

As I alluded to previously, there are in effect two types of self-awareness. One type concerns itself with knowledge of one's emotions, feelings, and desires. The other concerns itself with knowledge of one's cognitive processes such as what we know about things; how we do things; how we learn; how we solve problems; how we arrive at decisions; how effective our reasoning is, etc. The former can be referred to as emotional self-awareness and the latter as cognitive self-awareness. Emotional self-awareness is a component of emotional intelligence while cognitive self-awareness is a component of meta intelligence.

These two types of self-awareness are representative of the heart / mind dualism. I view them also as representative of the lower-brain vs higher-brain separation in that emotional self-awareness is concerned with controlling the primitive lower brain while cognitive self-awareness is concerned with developing the more recently evolved outer layers of the brain.

Some people may be inclined to focus on one type at the expense of the other. But this would be a mistake; you need both for full self-awareness and personal development. Having both emotional and cognitive awareness equips you to handle life's challenges with both hands rather than having one hand tied behind your back.

"We know the truth, not only by reason, but also by the heart."

-Blaise Pascal

I cannot overemphasise the power of self-awareness. It is the key to unlocking your potential. So, how can we use self-awareness to help us improve? To harness my self-awareness, I use what I call the 'ME & I' approach: Monitor,

Evaluate, & Improve. 'Me & I' is one variation of the analyze, evaluate, & create approach used by higher order thinkers. I 'ME & I' not only my cognitive processes but the habits and tools that improve those cognitive processes as well.

One indispensable tool that is central to the ME&I approach is a *journal*. By providing a recorded history, the journal enables us to monitor our thoughts over time. This allows us to see patterns in our thoughts and behaviors that might not otherwise have been apparent. It also allows us to focus on a particular cognitive process in order that we can evaluate its effectiveness. To evaluate something means to assess its value. At the most basic level we should evaluate whether something has a positive or negative impact on our lives.

"Truly it is an evil to be full of faults; but it is a still greater evil to be full of them and to be unwilling to recognize them."

-Blaise Pascal

*

Monitor your thoughts because they may turn into actions, and you can take back your thoughts, but you can't take back your actions.

*

———

—

"If it doesn't bring you joy, throw it out."

-Marie Kondo

Once we have monitored and evaluated an aspect of ourselves e.g. an attitude or behaviour, we are then in a position to manage it so that it improves our lives. To do this I use my MAD mental model – Modify, Add, or Delete. MAD is a general problem solving and decision-making method that recognizes that any thing or situation can be changed, removed, or supplemented. For example, when a given tool is not working for you, you can either fix it (modify), throw it out (delete), or get another tool (add). When we review our thinking patterns and habits, we may find that some of them are having a deleterious effect on our wellbeing. We can then take steps to remove them and optionally replace them with new empowering thoughts and habits.

For example, if we notice that we record the same negative thought patterns on a daily basis, we should obviously take steps to delete them from our lives. We can also add new positive thought patterns to replace them. If we notice that we are not achieving as many goals as we would like, then we can modify our goal setting skills. If we notice that we often feel stressed and anxious because of our poor financial state, we can delete that negative cognitive state by adding knowledge regarding investing. Optimizing our cognitive processes will give us more power to attain our goals and be successful. Think of it as feng shui for your mind. Create harmony for your mind by decluttering it and reorganizing it.

"The wisdom in life consists in the elimination of non-essentials."

-Lin Yutang

TAPPING YOUR INNER SHARK

So, what cognitive entities should we focus on to accomplish our goals? To attain the things I want in life, I develop and tap into my inner SHARK…

- **S**kills,
- **H**abits,
- **A**ttitudes,
- **R**esources,
- **K**nowledge.

I continuously analyze, evaluate, and improve these SHARK components in different areas of my life so that I can improve my thinking and in turn attain my goals in areas such as personal development, health, finance, relationships. This is my SHARK system for goal attainment. What you can attain in life is determined largely by the size of your shark. The bigger your shark, the bigger the goals you can achieve!

There are meta sharks and micro sharks. This book is an example of a meta shark i.e. a general shark that provides you with high-level skills, habits, attitudes, resources, and knowledge that can be used in all types of situations.

As you delve deeper into specific areas, your meta shark will spawn micro sharks that provide you with a more specific set of skills, habits, attitudes, resources, and knowledge that can be used to achieve success in those specific areas of life. Examples of micro sharks are financial sharks, career sharks, academic sharks, etc.

It is important to create a strong meta shark before attempting to create micro sharks. Doing so builds a solid cognitive foundation that will support any endeavor you attempt. A weak meta shark leads to weak micro sharks and short-lived successes. The sharks of meta intelligent successful people are more solid and richer than most. They are also constantly adapting and evolving.

In the next several chapters, I will explore the skills, habits, attitudes, resources, and knowledge of a strong meta shark.

"The ultimate value of life depends upon awareness and the power of contemplation rather than mere survival."

-Aristotle

CHAPTER 7:

META SKILLS

———

——

—

Having a strong skill set gives you the power to accomplish any task, project, or goal you set for yourself. The problem is that most people don't spend enough time working on their cognitive skills. They say they have no time, but ironically that's because they don't have the skills to make the most of their time.

To develop your meta shark, you need to develop not only your soft skills, but your meta skills as well. Meta skills are high level skills that generate and improve your overall skills. Being able to manage your skill set is an important skill in its own right. You need to know where your strengths and weaknesses lie, as well as prioritizing which skills or cognitive processes to develop. In this chapter, I list some MQ skills and cognitive processes that are worth 'ME & I' ing (monitoring, evaluating, & improving).

———

—

"The illiterate of the future will not be the person who cannot read. It will be the person who does not know how to learn, unlearn, and relearn."

-Alvin Toffler

The average person doesn't know how to learn effectively, and this is largely attributable to the ironic fact that school doesn't teach you *how* to learn. Even in university, I witnessed many students flounder because they didn't know how to study.

Another observation is that most people stop learning once they leave school. But once you stop learning, you stop growing. As former secretary of education, John W. Gardner lamented,

"I do worry about men and women functioning far below the level of their potential.

I'm talking about people who — no matter how busy they seem to be — have stopped learning or growing. Many of them are just going through the motions."

The problem is that most people don't view learning as a skill to be honed over a lifetime. And they also don't view learning as a priceless activity for life-long growth. This is truly a shame because we are fortunate to be living in the age of the internet where anyone can learn anything, anytime.

People need to take charge of their learning and teach themselves. They need to determine what things they must learn in order to achieve their goals and how to go about learning them.

*"Schools create conformity and kill creativity.
Your future depends on your capacity to teach yourself."*

-Russell Ackoff

The meta intelligentsia never stop learning, and moreover, they are *meta learners* who never stop learning how to learn. They constantly analyze, evaluate, and improve their learning strategies, techniques, etc.

"We need to stop thinking that we only acquire knowledge from 5 to 22 years old, and that then we can get a job and mentally coast through the rest of our lives if we work hard. To survive and thrive in this new era, we must constantly learn."

-Michael Simmons

Deliberate Learning

One useful strategy for learning is *deliberate learning*. This is Anders Ericsson's concept of *deliberate practice* applied to learning.

'Innate talent' is the IQ myth's analogue when it comes to excellence in fields like music and sports. Mozart is assumed to have been born with the gift of music. Many people take it for granted that Michael Jordan was blessed with 'God-given talent'. However, Ericsson's research has revealed that this is not the case. Achieving greatness takes practice - lots of practice! This is what led Malcolm Gladwell to propose his 10,000 hour rule: it takes 10K hours of practice to achieve excellence in a given field (Gladwell, 2008). Gladwell reached this conclusion based on Ericsson's research; however, Ericsson maintains that what is most important is not the quantity of practice, but rather the quality of practice - and deliberate practice is the best kind there is. (Ericsson & Pool, 2016)

"With the right kind of training, any individual will be able to acquire abilities that were previously viewed as only attainable if you had the right kind of genetic talent."

-Anders Ericsson

Deliberate practice is intense focused practice that attempts to improve, using continuous feedback, those areas of a skill which are suboptimal. This is in contrast to regular practice where often areas that have already been mastered are repeated (at the expense of weak areas) and practice sessions may be haphazard and lack any type of feedback mechanism.

The deliberate practice approach can be used to learn anything in general and Michael Simmons, who studies how successful people learn and think, has found that deliberate learning is the common thread amongst them. The uber successful like Gates, Buffett, & Musk schedule at least one focused hour each weekday for reading and learning. Simmons calls this the '5-hour rule'.

"Not learning at least 5 hours per week (the 5-hour rule) is the smoking of the 21st century."

-Michael Simmons

*

Persistent and focused practice makes anything possible, just like a stream cuts through rock to form a magnificent river canyon.

*

Smarter Learning

Smarter learning applies the SMARTER thinking method to the learning process. For example, the task or skill to be learned is regarded as a system to be broken down into its components. The components are then studied individually, and so too are their interrelationships.

An assessment of one's knowledge of the subject should be made prior, during, and after study. The gap between what one knows and needs to learn should be identified at all stages and strategies devised to close that gap.

Using constant feedback throughout the process, the learner identifies which strategies are working and which aren't. Impediments are identified and quickly dealt with.

Resources are marshalled to aid with the learning, such as relevant mental models, books, and the internet.

Unlearning

Not only do SMARTER thinkers know how to learn they also know how to *unlearn.* Few people realize that they must unlearn as much as they learn. We must unlearn because the world around us is constantly changing and consequently the mindset / mindware we use to represent it becomes obsolete and needs to be replaced with new beliefs, mental models, etc. Those who don't unlearn will not be able to adapt and will be at a constant disadvantage to those who do.

Unlearning is easier said than done because people are not inclined to introspect, and they are also averse to change. As Peter Senge advises …

"New insights fail to get put into practice because they conflict with deeply held internal images of how the world works … images that limit us to familiar ways of thinking and acting. That is why the discipline of managing mental models - surfacing, testing, and improving our internal pictures of how the world works - promises to be a breakthrough. Breakthroughs come when people learn how to take the time to stop and examine their assumptions."

———

—

Society tries to tell you *what* to think, but it is up to you to teach yourself *how* to think. The inability to think effectively can be very costly in all aspects of life. I previously discussed the higher-order and SMARTER thinking skills used by meta intelligent people. Now, I will discuss some other basic thinking techniques that everyone would be wise to learn.

CRITICAL THINKING

One basic thinking technique that everyone should know is *critical thinking*. There are various definitions of critical thinking, e.g. …

The ability to analyze information objectively and make a reasoned judgement.

-TheBalanceCareers.com

The key here is to *analyze objectively.* This means doing away with subjective forces like emotional biases which cloud your judgement. Emotional biases include ego preservation as well as prejudices based on nationalism, race, gender, age, etc.

There is a famous riddle that asks the following…

A father brings his injured son to the emergency room, but once there the E.R. surgeon exclaims, "I cannot operate on that boy, he is my son"! How can this be? The answer of course is that the surgeon is the boy's mother. People with a gender bias are usually stumped by this riddle.

If you can't completely eliminate your biases, you need to at least be aware of them, so that you know how they impact your thinking.

Another definition of critical thinking is…

The intellectually disciplined process of actively and skillfully conceptualizing, applying, analyzing, synthesizing, and/or evaluating information gathered from, or generated by, observation, experience, reflection, reasoning, or communication, as a guide to belief and action.

-CriticalThinking.org

Thus, critical thinking is a high-level skill that invokes other cognitive processes – analysis and evaluation in particular.

A central theme of critical thinking is that you shouldn't accept information, ideas, beliefs, assumptions, etc. at face value; you must objectively and rationally examine them in order to establish their veracity. Meta thinkers are critical thinkers that analyze and evaluate everything e.g. they not only scrutinize information, they also scrutinize the source of that information.

Critical thinking is now more important than ever because of the large volume of information that we are inundated with on the internet and social media platforms. And because we are living in the era of trolls and bots, a large part of that information may actually be misinformation or disinformation. We need critical thinking to determine what is real and not real.

"Beware of false knowledge.
It is more dangerous than ignorance."

-George Bernard Shaw

COMPUTATIONAL THINKING

Another technique that I find extremely useful is *computational thinking (CT)*. CT is a set of problem-solving methods that involve expressing problems and their solutions in ways a computer can execute.

Applied to everyday life, CT enables people to better understand and manage complex problems and systems.

Computational thinking is comprised of the following four stages …

1. Decomposition
2. Pattern recognition
3. Abstraction
4. Algorithm design

Each one of these components is an important thinking technique in its own right.

Decomposition

Decomposition involves decomposing a complex problem or system into smaller parts that are easier to understand. You can continue decomposing recursively until you arrive at parts that are small enough to manage.

Pattern Recognition

Pattern recognition entails finding similarities between the different parts that will help explain the whole.

Abstraction

This is a useful technique for dealing with complexity. Inconsequential details are filtered out and only the pertinent parts are kept, resulting in an abstracted model of the problem or system that is easier to understand and use. Abstraction is focusing on the important while simultaneously filtering out the unimportant.

Abstraction is another skill that is becoming more important due to an ever-increasing complex and info-centric society. The sheer volume of information available coupled with the lightening speed at which it is disseminated makes abstraction indispensable. Economist, Herbert A. Simon sums it up this way…

"What information consumes is rather obvious: it consumes the attention of its recipients. Hence a wealth of information creates a poverty of attention and a need to allocate that attention efficiently among the overabundance of information sources that might consume it."

Algorithm Design

In computer science, an algorithm is a set of precise instructions that enable a computer to do something such as solve a problem. Computers use algorithms; humans use plans. Use computational thinking to develop effective action plans that will take you from your present state to your goal state.

=-=-=

CT is considered by many to be a crucial thinking technique for the future. Here is what an article in *Wired*.com (09/2016) had to say about CT:

Computational thinking is going to be needed everywhere. And doing it well is going to be a key to success in almost all future careers.

—

*"It is remarkable how much long-term advantage people
like us have gotten by trying to be consistently not
stupid, instead of trying to be very intelligent."*

-Charlie Munger

In the same way that the average chess player can win more games by avoiding blunders rather than coming up with brilliant moves, the average person can fare better in life by avoiding thinking errors rather than coming up with brilliant ideas. This is Charlie Munger's *inversion* mental model applied to brilliance.

The first step in avoiding thinking errors is being able to identify them. There are several categories of thinking errors. The following are some of the more important and interesting ones…

- Cognitive biases
- Logical fallacies
- Rationalizations and 'Irrationalizations'
- Cognitive distortions

COGNITIVE BIASES

It was always assumed that most people behaved rationally but a psychologist / economist by the name of Daniel Kahneman showed that in fact people often behave irrationally. He was awarded the noble prize in economics (2002) for his work which spawned the study of cognitive biases and the field of behavioral economics. His book, *Thinking Fast and Slow*, is a summary of his research.

A cognitive bias is a systematic way of interpreting and processing information that leads to irrational judgement and decision-making. This corresponds to Kahneman's fast System 1 thinking which likes to use easy mental shortcuts (heuristics) as opposed to the more accurate but effortful & slow System 2 type of thinking.

There is nothing wrong with using System 1 for mundane tasks like choosing breakfast cereal; it is problematic when it is used for the more important decisions in life. Unfortunately, it seems many people don't spend any more time choosing a spouse e.g. than they do choosing a box of cereal.

There are dozens of cognitive biases. The following types are remarkably common…

Confirmation Bias

Confirmation bias is the tendency to look for, interpret, and recall information in a way that confirms one's pre-existing beliefs.

*

We don't see things as they are.
We see them as we would like them to be.

*

Individuals who exhibit confirmation bias tend to cite information that supports their views while dismissing information that does not align with them.

*"Don't waste your time with explanations:
people only hear what they want to hear."*

-Paulo Coelho

Hindsight Bias

Hindsght bias refers to the common tendency for people to perceive events that have already occurred as having been more predictable than they really were.

*"A stupid decision that works out well
becomes a brilliant decision in hindsight."*

-Daniel Kahneman

Availability Bias

The availability bias is the tendency to think that examples of things that come readily to mind are more representative than they really are.

The availability bias is important to know because advertisers, politicians, and others who are trying to influence your opinion may try to use it to their advantage. For example, they may strategically increase the frequency, recency, or salience of their message.

An important variant of the availability bias is the…

Repetition Bias

i.e. a cognitive bias in which there is a willingness to believe what we have been told most often and by the greatest number of sources.

-Psychology.wikia.org

This is true even if that information is false. Evil ideologues such as Adolf Hitler and his propaganda minister, Joseph Goebbels, took advantage of this bias in order to manipulate the German populace during their Nazi reign of terror. They called it *the big lie*.

*"If you tell a lie big enough and keep repeating it,
people will eventually come to believe it."*

-Joseph Goebbels

Today, malevolent agents have taken advantage of this bias together with technology to spread disinformation throughout social networks using internet bots.

Loss Aversion

Loss aversion refers to the tendency of people to prefer avoiding losses rather than acquiring equivalent gains, e.g. better not to lose money than make money. This bias often adversely impacts one's financial decisions.

=-=-=

The best remedy for cognitive biases (and thinking errors in general) is to develop cognitive self-awareness and constantly challenge your thinking, beliefs, and assumptions.

LOGICAL FALLACIES

A logical fallacy is simply an error in reasoning. Logical fallacies are similar to cognitive biases; the difference being that logical fallacies are a result of faulty argumentation as in the conclusion not following from the premise, whereas biases are predispositions towards a particular way of thinking.

Some examples of faulty logic include…

False Causation

The effect does not logically follow from the cause. This is one of the most widespread examples of irrational thought. People seem to have a tendency to illogically assume a causal link between two totally unrelated events, based solely on the fact that they occur close together in time.

This fallacy has many flavours…

Superstitious Thinking

Superstitious thinking is often a result of false causation that is based solely on coincidence. For example, an unrelated object is associated with a fortuitous event. The object then becomes your 'lucky charm'.

On the flip side, an object may become associated with a calamitous event, in which case the object becomes a 'curse' or 'jinx'. In some cases, the jinx was a person and the 'cursed' individual became ostracized by an entire group.

The problem with superstitious thinking is that by failing to identify the true cause of an event, you cannot effectively recreate the desired outcome or avoid the undesired outcome.

Magical Thinking

Magical thinking is the belief that one can influence external events through one's internal thoughts. For example, many people think that wishing for something will make it come true or that if you believe strongly enough in something, it will come true. Again, this is an example of an invalid cause and effect relationship. Sometimes a combination of coincidence and confirmation bias reinforces this type of thinking. For example, you wish for a new car and then an uncle suddenly dies leaving you a small inheritance which is just enough to pay for the car. From then on, you are convinced of the power of wishing.

=-=-=

Nowhere is superstition and magical thinking more prevalent than in the realm of sports. Players and fans alike have the strangest superstitions and rituals such as wearing the same 'lucky' clothes when their team plays. 'Lucky shorts' seem to be a popular charm. Michael Jordan had his favorite shorts and Jason Giambi wore a gold thong when he needed to break out of a hitting slump.

Magical thinking is also quite common among sports fans. They seem to think they can wish their team to victory.

Gambler's Fallacy

The gambler's fallacy is thinking that previous history affects current independent events. The classic example is the coin toss experiment. If a coin is tossed 9 times and lands heads each time, what is the probability that it will land heads the tenth time? The correct answer is 50%. If you said 0% you would be guilty of the gambler's fallacy (tails is due). If you said 100%, you would be guilty of the reverse gambler's fallacy (heads is favored).

RATIONALIZATIONS

A rationalization can be thought of as a seemingly logical justification for an unacceptable thought or action that avoids the real reasons behind the thought or action. Rationalization may occur consciously, or it may occur nonconsciously, in which case the rationalizer genuinely believes the rationalization. Deep feelings of shame may result in nonconscious rationalization. Cognitive dissonance may also lead to nonconscious rationalizing.

Cognitive dissonance refers to the psychological discomfort an individual may experience when they possess two contradictory thoughts. They may resort to rationalizing in order to reduce the dissonance.

Self-Deception Threshold

We are so good at fooling ourselves that we don't even realize it. Often people start out knowingly lying and rationalizing but then they reach a point where they start to believe their own lies and rationalizations. I call this point: the *self-deception threshold*.

"Nothing fools you better than the lie you tell yourself."

-Teller

Sour Grapes Rationalization

A famous example of rationalization was provided by Aesop in one of his fables, 'The Fox and the Grapes'. After trying unsuccessfully to reach a bunch of grapes, the fox then declares them to be undesirable because they are sour.

Individuals often minimize the positives and accentuate the negatives of something (or someone) they desired but were unable to attain. As a testament to how common this type of rationalization is, the phrase 'sour grapes' has worked it's way into the popular lexicon.

IRRATIONALIZATIONS

Irrationalization is the term I use for an 'irrational rationalization'. If rationalizations are rational justifications for questionable thoughts or behavior, then irrationalizations are irrational justifications for questionable thoughts or behavior. And where rationalizations offer plausible reasons, irrationalizations offer implausible if not downright ludicrous reasons.

Irrationalization is demonstrated by the…

Broken Biscuit Effect

which derives its name from the irrational notion that 'broken biscuits have no calories', which a dieting person will cite before consuming a broken biscuit.

-HowToGetYourOwnWay.com

=-=-=

Irrationalizations are more common than you might think - especially when the perpetrator must quickly think of an excuse to get out of doing something. E.g. "I can't go out with you because I don't like your shoes."

COGNITIVE DISTORTIONS

"Men are disturbed not by things, but by the view which they take of them."

-Epictetus

A cognitive distortion is irrational thinking that causes an individual to perceive reality inaccurately. The concept of cognitive distortions and cognitive therapy was developed by psychiatrist Aaron Beck in the 1960s & 1970s as a quicker and more effective alternative to traditional Freudian psychotherapy in the treatment of psychologically dysfunctional individuals.

But here's the thing – 'functional' individuals can experience cognitive distortions as well, just not nearly to the same frequency and degree as the mentally ill. In any event, everyone can make use of the cognitive therapy approach, namely the identification and challenging of negative thoughts responsible for negative emotions and behaviours.

Recognizing and labeling negative thoughts is helpful because like they say: "if you can name it, you can tame it".

We can go even one step further and identify and evaluate all our thoughts (not just dysfunctional ones) with the aim of improving them. Optimizing our thoughts in this way is an important facet of meta intelligence.

The following cognitive distortions are surprisingly quite common in the general population…

All or Nothing Thinking

This is when you view everything as being either black or white with no shades of gray in between. You are either a complete failure or a total success. Other people are either all good or all bad.

The antidote for this binary type of thinking is *fuzzy logic thinking*. Fuzzy logic thinking is a non-binary way of thinking. Instead of true or false, something could be partly true & partly false. Instead of all or nothing of something, it could be some part of it. Fuzzy logic thinking means not thinking in polarized terms. It's being able to see the full spectrum of colors.

As people evolve intellectually, their thinking becomes more nuanced. For example, they no longer simply see people as being exclusively good or bad; they see people as having a mixture of both good and bad traits.

Overgeneralization

Overgeneralization is a dysfunctional way of thinking that makes a self-limiting all-encompassing generalization based on a single negative experience. This often occurs when someone's romantic overtures are rebuffed. The individual then believes that nobody will ever love them and that they are destined to be alone for the rest of their lives. This can also occur in more subtle ways such as letting a single failure stop us from pursuing our dreams.

Jumping to Conclusions (JTC)

JTC is when we conclude something without adequate evidence. JTC is usually associated with negative conclusions but the opposite can also occur where the individual creates a favourable but unrealistic expectation. This latter type is responsible for many business failures and crushing disappointments.

Two common subtypes of JTC are:

- Fortune-telling (anticipating a situation will turn out badly)

- Mind-reading (anticipating people will think negatively of
  you)

PROBABILISTIC THINKING

Committing the thinking errors I've listed can have
serious consequences such as bankruptcy, depression, and
gambling addiction. A good way to minimize thinking errors is
to learn some basic probability theory and to adopt a
probabilistic way of thinking.

"Research has shown that even relatively basic training in
probability makes people better forecasters and helps them
avoid certain cognitive biases."

-Walter Frick (Harvard Business Review)

Probabilistic thinking combines knowledge of
probability with logic to estimate the likelihood of an event
occurring.

"I look at the future from the standpoint of probabilities. It's like a branching stream of probabilities, and there are actions that we can take that affect those probabilities."

-Elon Musk

———

—

The following skills have taken on increasing importance in today's rapidly changing and complex world. Meta thinkers master these skills in order to stay on top of change and complexity.

- Goal setting
- Risk management
- Problem solving & decision making
- Adaptability
- Time management

GOAL SETTING

Goals provide direction for our lives. Without goals, we run amok like the proverbial chicken without a head. Success scholar, Brian Tracy has been studying successful individuals for decades, and he is convinced that a large part of their success is due to them being goal oriented.

Some techniques that can help you in setting your goals include the W5 and 5Whys techniques which I discussed when describing root cause analysis. Another technique is the SMART goal-setting system. The SMART system is a terrific time-tested technique for setting goals. SMART goals should be…

- **S**pecific (clear)
- **M**easurable (to track your progress)
- **A**chievable (doable)
- **R**elevant (meaningful for you)
- **T**imely (have a time target and track your time)

The SMART system is great for most goals; however, if you want to accomplish something truly spectacular, then you might want to set goals that appear to be beyond your reach. Setting only small goals for yourself often leads to big regrets later in life.

"Don't be on your deathbed someday, having squandered your one chance at life, full of regret because you pursued little distractions instead of big dreams."

-Derek Sivers

For your big goals you can use my SHARK system for goal attainment: determine and write down all the skills, habits, attitudes, resources, & knowledge that will be necessary to achieve your goal. This will then serve as your handbook for that goal.

"The greater danger for most of us lies not in setting our aim too high and falling short; but in setting our aim too low and achieving our mark."

-Michelangelo

*

If you're not failing at something,

you haven't challenged yourself enough.

*

RISK MANAGEMENT

It is important to be able to detect land mines that may lie on your path towards a given goal. I use my IED acronym as a reminder to…

- *I*dentify potential problems
- *E*valuate their likelihood and impact
- *D*ecide how to handle them
  Depending on my evaluation, I can choose to ignore, remove, or mitigate them.

"Whatever can go wrong, will go wrong."

-Murphy's Law

PROBLEM SOLVING & DECISION MAKING

There is no such thing as a problem-free life. In order to be successful, we must have the ability to effectively solve problems and decide on the correct course of action to take. You will find many excellent problem-solving / decision-making methods in the literature. A simple and effective method is…

- Analyze and understand the problem
- Form candidate solutions

- Evaluate the candidate solutions
- Decide which solution will best meet your needs

I would just add that sometimes you can select two or more complementary solutions and act on them simultaneously as is the case with the familiar problem of how to lose weight: diet and exercise.

=-=-=

When making decisions, it is important to take into consideration *opportunity cost* and to not take into consideration *sunk cost*.

Opportunity cost refers to the loss of potential gain from other alternatives when one alternative is chosen.

*

Remember that whenever you decide to do something, you have decided not to do something else.

*

Sunk cost refers to a cost that has already been incurred and cannot be recovered. A sunk cost should never be a consideration for any future decision-making, but due in large part to the loss aversion bias, it frequently is. This is known as the *sunk cost effect*. A common example of this effect would be sitting through a movie you did not enjoy solely because 'you had already paid for it'.

=-=-=

Ineffective decision making often results from these types of thinking errors. It may also result from not accurately determining the parameters of the problem or failing to look at all the possible alternatives (*alternative blindness,* (Dobelli, 2013)). But as Rolf Dobelli advises in his book, *The Art of Thinking Clearly,* sometimes you need to strike a balance between considering too few possibilities and too many. Too many options can lead to bad decisions as well. Sometimes, we are presented with them (*the paradox of choice*) and sometimes we seek them out (information bias). (Dobelli, 2013)

*

A wealth of information can create a mass of confusion.

*

*"A man with a watch knows what time it is.
A man with two watches is never sure."*

-Segal's Law

ADAPTABILITY

*"Change is the law of life. And those who look only
to the past or present are certain to miss the future."*

-John F. Kennedy

Adaptability can be variously defined as...

- How well one can adapt to change
- The ability to adjust to changing circumstances
- The ability to effectively change course when faced with a new situation.

Being able to adapt is of course highly dependent on your *adaptive thinking* skills, but your other SMARTER thinking skills and higher-order thinking skills also come into play. You also need a mindset that is conducive to change.

The inability to adjust to changing circumstances can result in *learned helplessness* as described by Stephen Covey in the following passage:

"Our personal environment is also changing at an ever-increasing pace. Such rapid change burns out a large number of people who feel they can hardly handle it, can hardly cope with life. They become reactive and essentially give up, hoping that the things that happen to them will be good."

(Covey, 1989)

But before we can adapt to change, we need to be able to detect it, and how quickly we can detect change can be just as important as how well we adapt to it. I see three different scenarios…

In the ideal scenario, you can foresee change and are prepared in advance for it.

In the next best scenario, you fail to foresee change, but can quickly change direction when it happens.

The worst-case scenario is when you fail to foresee change and don't react quickly enough when it is upon you.

In the business world, failure to adapt to new technology can spell doom for a company. Blockbuster Video is a prime example of this.

"It is not the strongest of the species that survive, nor the most intelligent, but the ones most responsive to change."

-Charles Darwin

TIME MANAGEMENT

"A man who dares to waste one hour of time has not discovered the value of life."

-Charles Darwin

There is nothing more precious than time. Money is infinite, but time is finite. So, you must manage your time wisely, not waste it.

Time management is the process of planning and controlling the amount of time we spend on specific activities.

Good time management increases efficiency and productivity. Poor time management leads to increased stress and loss of control.

*

How much do you value your life?

That is how much you should value your time,

for they are one and the same.

To waste time is to waste your life.

*

There are various tools relating to time management. One famous tool is attributed to Dwight D. Eisenhower and is referred to as the Eisenhower Matrix (or Eisenhower Box). Eisenhower was a former U.S. general and president, so he should know a thing or two about managing time. Eisenhower's matrix lets you prioritize and process tasks based on urgency and importance.

The Eisenhower Decision Matrix

Luxafor.com

The Eisenhower matrix yields the following four types of tasks as well as the corresponding 4 D's of action…

1. Urgent and important – Do

2. Important but not urgent – Defer

3. Urgent but not important – Delegate

4. Neither urgent nor important – Delete

You should only concern yourself with important tasks. Unimportant tasks can be delegated or ignored. Once you have dealt with the important emergencies of the first quadrant, you are then free to work on the empowering growth activities of the second quadrant. As Stephen Covey advised in his classic book, *The 7 Habits of Highly Effective People* (Covey, 1989), meta thinkers spend most of their time in the second quadrant; that is where the opportunities for internal as well as external growth lie.

*

Just as it is important to know the things you should be doing,

it is equally important to know the things you shouldn't be doing.

*

The E senhower Matrix can be used in conjunction with that most basic yet useful of time management tools – the to-do list. And it's also useful to have a not-to-do list. Conduct a time audit for yourself to see which of your activities do not contribute to your goals – these are your time wasters, then put them on your not-to-do list.

*"The most precious resource we all have is time.
Do not waste it living someone else's life."*

-Steve Jobs

Chapter 8:

Meta Habits

———
——
—

"We are what we repeatedly do.
Excellence, then, is not an act but a habit."

-Will Durant

Habits are important because of their cumulative impact on our lives. Good habits will lead to a satisfying life; bad habits will slowly but surely erode the quality of your life. And because they occur frequently, habits become automatic thus necessitating the need to manage them through self-awareness.

Success researchers such as Tom Corley (*Rich Habits*) and Tim Ferriss (*Tools of Titans*) have extensively studied and written about the habits of successful people. You should devour their books and any other books or blogs on this topic – they are absolute gold!

In this chapter, I will discuss some of the more useful habits you should adopt to be more successful.

*

The road to success is paved with good habits.

*

THE 8 HABITS OF HIGHLY META INTELLIGENT

PEOPLE

———

—

There are many good habits one can follow; however, I consider the following habits to be the core meta intelligent habits because they are what most distinguishes the meta intelligentsia from other folk. If practiced daily, they will guarantee personal mastery and success. I call them *the 8 habits of highly meta intelligent people*. They have been as valuable to me as gold and I am sure you will TREASURE them as well…

1. **T**hink of ways to improve
2. **R**eview your goals
3. **E**ducate yourself
4. **A**sk questions
5. **S**elf-reflect
6. **U**se a journal
7. **R**ise early and start your morning ritual
8. **E**xercise your mind as well as your body

THINK OF WAYS TO IMPROVE

"Challenge yourself everyday to be better and do better. Remember, growth starts with a decision to move beyond your present circumstances."

-Robert Tew

Everyone should strive to be the best person that they can be. That, to me, is the essence of being human and I cannot fathom why so many people are apparently satisfied with not reaching their full potential.

"There is nothing noble in being superior to your fellow man; true nobility is being superior to your former self."

-Ernest Hemingway

REVIEW YOUR GOALS

Goals, especially life goals, are the motivational carrot that keeps moving us forward. Goals are also important for providing focus. Without goals, we either stagnate or wander around aimlessly.

*"The person who makes a success of living is the one
who sees his goal steadily and aims for it unswervingly."*

-Cecil B. DeMille

EDUCATE YOURSELF

*"The man who has not the habit of
reading is imprisoned in his immediate
world."*

-Lin Yutang

Most people stop learning the day they graduate from school while meta thinkers never stop learning; in fact, they like to learn something new every day!

Meta thinkers are autodidactic – they don't need anybody to teach them, they teach themselves. Reading is of course a prime way of educating yourself, but I purposely did not title this section *read* because in today's techno-centric society there are many different options for learning such as webinars, podcasts, TED talks, learning apps, YouTube videos, etc.

And you don't have to restrict yourself to the paper version of your favourite book either – you can read an eBook or listen to an audio book (audio books are great when driving or working out). It's a similar story for magazines and newspapers – you can get them online. Nor do you have to go to a physical class to take a course – you can do that online too.

What's more important than the tool you use to acquire information is the type of information you acquire. That's another reason why I didn't title this section simply 'read'. Reading trash tabloids etc. won't help your intellectual development. Meta intelligent people are selective about what information they absorb, choosing to focus on educational material that will help them grow and help them achieve their goals. Bill Gates and Warren Buffett are famous voracious readers and a large part of their day is dedicated to reading material that will enhance their knowledge.

> *"Formal education will make you a living.*
> *Self-education will make you a fortune."*
>
> -Jim Rohn

ASK QUESTIONS

"Quality questions create a quality life."
*"Successful people ask better questions and as a
result, they get better answers."*

-Tony Robbins

Only fools believe they have all the answers. Most people probably realize they don't have all the answers, but they are satisfied with the answers they do have. Meta thinkers, on the other hand, are never satisfied - they are always asking new questions and looking for new answers.

*"Often, all that stands between you and
what you want is a better set of questions."*

-Tim Ferriss

SELF-REFLECT

A wonderful example of self-reflection is provided to us by Charles Dickens' *A Christmas Carol*. It is ultimately the story of one flawed man's journey of self-reflection and eventual enlightenment. Ebenezer Scrooge is a selfish tightwad but one night he is visited by the ghosts of Christmas past, present, and future. Through the ghosts he is able to see his miserly ways and the sad fate that awaits him if he doesn't change.

Great philosophers throughout history have been advocates of daily self-reflection. Seneca described his self-reflection this way…

> "When the light has been removed and my wife has fallen silent, aware of this habit that's now mine, I examine my entire day and go back over what I've done and said, hiding nothing from myself, passing nothing by.
>
> For why should I fear any consequence from my mistakes, when I'm able to say, 'See that you don't do it again, but now I forgive you.'"

"Every night before going to sleep, we must ask ourselves: what weakness did I overcome, what virtue did I acquire?"

-Seneca

This type of reflection at the end of the day is typical of many successful people and forms part of their *evening ritual*.

USE A JOURNAL

It is not an exaggeration to say that my life turned around once I started using a journal. By recording my thoughts and actions, I could later analyze, evaluate, & improve them.

You can use a journal in many ways and tailor it to your individual needs. For example, I also use my journal for jotting down my ideas and goals.

Another way I use my journal is for conducting post-mortems when my projects don't go as planned. I identify and record all the root causes of the problems encountered. I then write down the solutions as well as the *lessons learnt* for the future.

But I also make a note of things that worked. I try to identify the underlying principles that made it work and see if I can apply those principles to other areas and eventually incorporate them into one of my *personal success systems*.

RISE EARLY AND START YOUR MORNING RITUAL

"You'll never change your life until you change something you do daily. The secret of your success is found in your daily routine."

-John C. Maxwell

The average person typically gets up at the last minute, takes a quick shower, grabs a quick bite – if they have time, and rushes off to the office where they half-heartedly go through the motions of their job. Top performers, on the other hand, make it a habit to get up early to get a head start on their day. They also set aside time every morning for activities (such as the habits discussed in this chapter) that will leave them motivated and energized for the rest of the day. The amount of time allotted can be anywhere from a couple of minutes to a couple of hours, although it's usually between 30 - 90 minutes. These early morning routines are exceedingly popular among successful people and are known as *morning rituals*.

Some early risers include …

Tim Cook, the Apple CEO, wakes up at 3:45am every morning. He checks his email for about an hour, and then hits the gym. After his workout, he gets a cup of coffee at Starbucks and heads to the office.

Bob Iger, the Disney CEO, is an early riser too. He wakes up at 4:30am each day and reads the papers, listens to music, exercises, checks emails and watches TV.

-www.thewisdompost.com

Of course, there is no magic hour at which you should get up. That depends on everyone's personal circumstances. Moreover, everybody's morning ritual is different, depending on what inspires them.

Tony Robbins uses a ritual called *priming*:

1. Perform three sets of 30 Kapalbhati Pranayama breaths.
2. Close your eyes and slow your breathing while expressing gratitude for everything you have.
3. Pray and ask for help, guidance, and strength throughout the day.

Tim Ferriss adapted his own morning ritual after interviewing thousands of successful leaders from all walks of life.

First, Ferriss makes his bed. He says it fills him with a small sense of pride and accomplishes something right away.

Next, he meditates for 10 to 20 minutes; then does at least 30 minutes of exercise followed by some strong tea.

He finishes his routine by journaling for 5 to 10 minutes, which helps him "push the ball forward and feel better throughout the day."

Oprah Winfrey starts her morning with 20 minutes of meditation, which she says fills her with "hope, a sense of contentment and deep joy."

Next, she hits the treadmill to get her heart-rate pumping. Winfrey swears that at least 15 minutes of exercise improves her productivity and boosts energy levels.

Next, Winfrey "tunes herself in" by going for a walk, listening to music or preparing a nice meal. She always concludes her ritual by eating a healthy meal full of complex carbohydrates, fiber and protein.

-www.inc.com

Many successful people also include the following as part of their morning routine.

- Meditate / Contemplate
- Set goals and plan
- Work towards their passion and purpose

My own morning ritual consists of sitting down in front of my laptop, enjoying my latte as I …

- read articles about successful people and what they did to become successful. (This provides inspiration as well as education)
- Brainstorm ideas for creativity projects.
- Brainstorm ideas for business projects.
- Review and set goals.
- Plan the day's activities.

I then take my dog for a walk (which provides exercise and fresh air) and I start to work on my ideas as soon as I get back.

*

Improving your life begins with improving your daily habits.

*

EXERCISE YOUR MIND AS WELL AS YOUR BODY

Most people are aware of the benefits of physical exercise and that's great, but many are not aware of the benefits of mental exercise. Meta thinkers are always engaged in cerebral activities of one kind or another. This develops your mind by exposing you to new problems and solutions, as well as new ideas and strategies.

Some mental exercises include…

- Write (book, blog, etc.)
- Take up a creative hobby e.g. music or art
- Play challenging strategy games e.g. chess
- Study difficult subjects
- Tackle a difficult project
- Learn new things
- Do logic, math, crossword puzzles etc.
- Debate

- Play the devil's advocate

The following are some of the things I do to challenge myself and keep my mind sharp. They also happen to be hobbies I enjoy and make my life more interesting.

- I write.
- I dabble with the guitar and piano.
- I like to learn different languages and practice with the locals.
- I read scientific articles on disparate subjects.
- I play chess and other strategy games.

Chess has taught me some valuable life lessons such as the importance of planning several moves ahead as well as constantly challenging yourself. For example, a well-known maxim in chess is that you won't improve until you play stronger opponents! So, I always try to find increasingly harder challenges for myself. I also try to associate with highly meta intelligent people.

Stretch your comfort zone

"Everything you want is just outside your comfort zone."

-Robert Allen

You should try to do things outside of your comfort zone. This will accelerate your growth. Amy Poehler has a beautiful take on this…

Great people do things before they're ready. They do things before they know they can do it. Doing what you're afraid of, getting out of your comfort zone, taking risks like that – that is what life s. You might be really good. You might find out something about yourself that's really special, and if you're not good, who cares? You tried something. Now you know something about yourself.

"Unless you try to do something beyond what you have already mastered, you will never grow."

-Ronald E. Osborn

GOOD HABITS THAT MAY ACTUALLY BE BAD FOR

YOU

———

—

- **Positive thinking**

To be frank, there is bad positive thinking and there is good positive thinking. I will discuss the bad kind here and the good kind in the next chapter.

Bad positive thinking is woo-woo positive thinking such as expecting to receive things without putting in the work needed to obtain them. This type of entitled positive thinking is quite common and I think part of the reason for this is because people are vulnerable to the thinking errors I described previously (magical thinking springs immediately to mind).

Woo-woo positive thinking is bad because it leads to laziness, entitlement, and a dreamer mentality where the individual believes they don't have to plan or take action.

Beloved comedic actor, Jim Carrey, is often touted as an example of the power of the *manifestation mindset*, however this is misguided because before he became an 'overnight sensation', he had honed his craft working small gigs for many years. In fact, Jim Carrey, himself, advises:

"You can't visualize and then go eat a sandwich."

This situation is typical of *manifester's* 'success' stories. After all, Rhonda Byrne didn't just sit around staring at her vision board – she wrote a book about it!

• Keeping your nose to the grindstone

This habit may cause you to miss out on opportunities and on life.

"Those who are wise won't be busy;
those who are too busy can't be wise."

-Lin Yutang

"Life is too short to be busy."

-Tim Ferriss

• Being agreeable

Be careful about being **too** nice. You don't want to be a doormat. Always saying yes to people will cause you to be overextended and may lead to burn out.

Derek Sivers achieved fame and fortune with his CD Baby platform for indie musicians, but he realized he was agreeing to do many things out of a sense of obligation with the negative consequence that he was overcommitting himself and feeling drained. This led him to develop his famous "hell yeah" philosophy …

If you're not saying, 'HELL YEAH!' about something, say 'no'. If you feel anything less than Wow! That would be amazing! Hell Yeah! Then say 'no'. When you say no to most things, you leave room in your life to really throw yourself completely into that rare thing that makes you say, 'HELL YEAH!'

(Sivers, 2011)

- **Analyzing all the facts**

According to Jeff Bezos, most decisions should be made with around 70% of the information needed. Waiting for more information will just slow you down.

> *"If you spend too much time thinking about a thing, you will never get it done."*
>
> -Bruce Lee

- **Meticulous planning**

You need to be flexible.

> *"I couldn't live by a rigid schedule. I try to live freely from moment to moment, letting things happen and adjusting to them."*
>
> -Bruce Lee

BAD HABITS THAT MAY NOT BE SO BAD AFTER ALL

———

—

- **Watching tv (or Netflix etc.)**

There is plenty of intelligent programming out there. The problem is that people just watch the junk and they spend too much time watching tv.

- **Internet surfing**

Like television, there is plenty of good content and plenty of bad content. I personally regard the internet as an indispensable learning resource. There are also exceptionally good meta intelligent bloggers out there like Shane Parrish (Farnam Street), Michael Simmons (Mental Model Club), and James Clear who I regularly follow.

- **Taking many risks**

"In a world that's constantly changing quickly, the only strategy that is guaranteed to fail is not taking any risks."

-Mark Zuckerberg

"You miss 100% of the shots you don't take."

-Wayne Gretzky

The average person is brought up to 'play it safe', 'don't take any chances'. But, is that the way you really want to live your life? A life of mediocrity? The following powerful passage from Theodore Roosevelt's *Man in the Arena* speech is very inspiring.

"The credit belongs to the man who is actually in the arena; whose face is marred by the dust and sweat and blood; who strives valiantly ... who, at worst, if he fails, at least fails while daring greatly; so that his place shall never be with those cold and timid souls who know neither victory or defeat."

Sure, you might fall flat on your face, but that's okay, because you will learn from the experience. Until you view adversity as necessary for growth, you will not have the courage to take risks.

*

**Failure is not the antithesis of success.
It is in fact a necessary ingredient in any recipe for success.**

*

———

——

The following habits will suck the soul right out of you…

- **Working at something you hate / Not doing what you love**

"I never did a day's work in my life. It was all fun."

-Thomas Edison

It is difficult to imagine that the majority of people will spend their lives working at something they do not enjoy. Consequently, they will have died long before they are buried.

Always remember that you are not bound to your present circumstances. If you don't like what you're doing, do something else, for as George Burns advised:

"It is better to be a failure at something you love than to be a success at something you hate."

*

If you are not living with passion, you are not living.

*

- **Self-reproach and recrimination**

"You are your own worst critic."

-Anonymous

Blaming yourself won't get you anywhere but forgiving yourself will take you a very long way.

- **Dwelling on the past and being full of regret**

If we spend all our time dwelling on the past and worrying about the future, we won't have time to enjoy the present.

- **Fearing the future and the unknown**

The best way to prepare for the future is to focus on succeeding today, which also happens to be the best way to forget about the past.

"If you are depressed, you are living in the past.
If you are anxious, you are living in the future.
If you are at peace, you are living in the
present."

-Lao Tzu

- **Fearing failure**

Many luminaries have written about failure and its importance for growth. Leadership guru, John C. Maxwell calls this 'failing forward' and he has devoted a whole book to the subject (Maxwell, Failing Forward: Turning mistakes into stepping stones for success, 2007). Maxwell's premise is that the main difference between average people and achievers is their perception of and response to failure.

He writes…

> There is no achievement without failure.
> Embrace adversity and make failure a regular part of your life. If you're not failing, you're probably not really moving forward.
> Fail early, fail often, but always fail forward!

"It is impossible to live without failing at something, unless you live so cautiously that you might as well not have lived at all."

-J.K. Rowling

CHAPTER 9:

META ATTITUDES

———

——

—

*"A bad attitude is like a flat tire: you can't
go anywhere without changing it."*

-Anonymous

ttitudes are especially important in determining your destiny because they occur to a large extent at a nonconscious level and are constantly operating in the background. This is why self-awareness is so important in that it brings them to the surface where we can consciously manage them.

The following attitudes are essential to personal mastery and success and constitute the foundation of the meta intelligent mindset.

- Positive
- Internal locus of control
- Can-Do
- Continuous improvement
- Persistent
- Resilient
- Curious
- Creative
- Open-minded
- Flexible
- Independent

Some people may regard attitudes such as these to be innate personality traits, but this is a mistaken and self-limiting belief. They are in fact cognitive processes that can be learned by anyone.

"The greatest discovery of my generation is that human beings can alter their lives by altering their attitudes of mind."

-William James

POSITIVE

"Whether you think you can or think you can't, you're right."

-Henry Ford

Here, I am talking about realistic positive thinking, and not the woo-woo positive thinking I described in the previous chapter.

A positive but pragmatic attitude allows you to see and act on opportunities where others see only problems. It allows you to see possibilities where negative people see only impossibility.

The average person views failure as something negative. Meta intelligent people, on the other hand, view failure as a valuable lesson that will take them one step further towards their goal as did Thomas Edison when he was inventing the light bulb.

Having a positive attitude is vital because it determines your approach to life. It also determines how much you will grow.

*

Winners create results.

Losers create excuses.

*

INTERNAL LOCUS OF CONTROL

"It is not in the stars to hold our destiny, but in ourselves."

-Shakespeare

Locus of control refers to the degree with which people believe they have control over events in their lives. People who have an internal locus believe they are in control of their life. People who have an external locus believe there are external forces beyond their control.

*

Our lives are shaped by the choices we make.

To improve your life, begin by accepting responsibility for it.

*

In extreme cases of external locus, individuals suffer from learned helplessness i.e. they believe that nothing they do can improve their situation. The opposite is true of people with high internal locus of control. They believe they have the power to create whatever situation they want. Nobody exemplifies this better than Oprah Winfrey. As Oprah relates in the following passage, she overcame difficult circumstances to become one of the most successful women in history…

What I learned at a very young age was that I was responsible for my life.

You cannot blame apartheid, your parents, or your circumstances because you are not your circumstances. You are your possibilities. If you know that, you can do anything.

"You alone paint your own canvas,
thought by thought, choice by choice."

-Oprah Winfrey

An internal locus of control enables you to be proactive and grab the bull by the horns. With an external locus of control, you will be reactive and go through life like a pinball, bouncing off one bumper to another.

*

Winners make things happen.
Losers let things happen to them.

*

People with an internal locus always take responsibility for their life and their actions. People with an external locus, on the other hand, refuse to take responsibility. They prefer to indulge in the *blame game* – searching for scapegoats to absolve themselves of responsibility.

When they're not playing the blame game, externally oriented people are busy playing the victim game. Instead of doing something about their misfortune, they wallow in it. Sometimes life does land you cruel blows but meta intelligent individuals know that even though they may not be responsible for hardships thrown their way, they are most definitely responsible for how they deal with them.

*

Blaming something or someone for your problems will not fix them. Ultimately it is up to you to overcome any difficulties you face.

*

CAN-DO

"Impossible is not a fact. It's an opinion."

-Muhammad Ali

When you combine a positive attitude with an internal locus of control you have the Can-Do attitude – the belief that you can do anything if you set your mind to it. This attitude allows you to achieve successes; successful experiences, in turn, strengthen your can-do attitude in a virtuous cycle.

"Doubt kills more dreams than failure ever will."

-Suzy Kassem

CONTINUOUS IMPROVEMENT

"Continuous improvement is better than delayed perfection."

-Mark Twain

One of the hallmarks of successful people in any field is that they are always striving to improve themselves. For example, I was always impressed by the fact that the greatest athletes of their sport (e.g. Michael Jordan, Wayne Gretzky, Cristiano Ronaldo) were never content to rest on their laurels. Despite the fact they were at the top of their game, they still constantly strived for small improvements in their skills.

"If you think you're already perfect, then you never will be."

-Cristiano Ronaldo

The Japanese understand the resultant power of making small daily improvements in every facet of their lives. This concept is known as Kaizen and it figures predominantly in Japanese culture. In fact, Toyota used it to great effect in becoming the world's number one automobile maker. Their method became known as the *Toyota way* and it has served as a model for corporations and individuals alike.

Tony Robbins is a big proponent of kaizen. Regrettably, there is no equivalent word in English, which is why Robbins created his CANI mnemonic - Constant And Never-ending Improvement. (Robbins, Awaken the Giant Within, 1991). Robbins is adamant that the level of success we achieve is directly proportional to our commitment to CANI, and I couldn't agree more.

Your evolution is proportional to your motivation to constantly change:

$$E=MC^2$$

Evolution = Motivation * Constant Change

PERSISTENT

"To follow without halt one aim:
That is the secret of success."

-Anna Pavlova

Meta intelligent people are persistent. They always set goals for themselves and they don't stop until they reach them.

*"Being defeated is often a temporary condition.
Giving up is what makes it permanent."*

-Marilyn Vos Savant

RESILIENT

*'Our greatest glory is not in never failing,
but in rising every time we fail."*

-Nelson Mandela

"Fall seven times, stand up eight."

-Japanese proverb

Meta intelligent people are very resilient. They are undeterred by setbacks. They know that you only fail when you quit and that the secret to success is to learn from your mistakes and keep going.

Many people, on the other hand, do not handle failure very well. They see failure as something terrible that should be avoided at all costs. If they fail, they see themselves as failures. Their attitude prevents them from learning from their mistakes and so they are destined to repeat them.

In the end, it is not whether we fail that matters. What is important is how we respond to failure, for that is what will shape our character and ultimately our destiny.

*

The only way to avoid making mistakes is to avoid doing anything.

*

"Failure is simply the opportunity to begin again, this time more intelligently."

-Henry Ford

"Success is 99% failure."

-Soichiro Honda

*

There is nothing wrong in falling down. There is a problem, however, in not having the will to get back up.

*

CURIOUS

"Curiosity is, in great and generous minds, the first passion and the last."

-Samuel Johnson

Meta thinkers are interminably curious about everything. They are naturally inquisitive – always pondering the universe and asking questions. They want to know how things work and why they are the way they are. They are perpetually trying new ways of doing things.

*

If you don't try anything new, you don't learn anything new.

*

The meta intelligent are polymaths who are passionate about learning multiple subjects. Being knowledgeable in many fields allows one to integrate diverse perspectives. It also acts as a hedge against downturns in individual sectors of the economy. This diversified knowledge allows polymaths to be what Nassim Taleb describes as *antifragile* (Taleb, 2012). While specialists are vulnerable to disruption, polymaths thrive with change.

It is useful to bear in mind that the greatest thinkers in history were all polymaths: Da Vinci, Newton, Darwin, Edison, Franklin, etc. And it is noteworthy as well that the most successful people today are also polymaths: e.g. Bezos, Gates, Buffet, Musk.

CREATIVE

"Creation is a drug I can't do without!"

-Cecil B. DeMille

Creativity is the extension of curiosity. Being open to new experiences and new ways of thinking lends itself to creative output. As Steve Jobs explained, *"creative people are able to connect experiences and synthesize new things."*

OPEN-MINDED

"A mind is like a parachute. It doesn't work if it is not open."

-Frank Zappa

The minds of meta thinkers are always open to entertaining different viewpoints. This is an extremely important attitude to have because having a closed mind impedes one's ability to learn and improve.

"It is the mark of an educated mind to be able to entertain a thought without accepting it."

-Aristotle

Charles Darwin was renowned for his open-mindedness; he called it his *golden rule*:

"I had, also, during many years, followed a golden rule, namely, that whenever a published fact, a new observation or thought came across me, which was opposed to my general results, to make a memorandum of it without fail and at once."

Undoubtedly channeling Darwin, Charlie Munger had this to say:

"You must understand the opposite side of the argument better than the person holding that side does. It's a very difficult way to think, tremendously unnatural in the face of our genetic makeup (the more typical response is to look for as much confirming evidence as possible). Harnessed properly, though, it is a powerful way to beat your own shortcomings and become a seeing man amongst the blind."

FLEXIBLE

*"Those who cannot change their
minds, cannot change anything."*

-George Bernard Shaw

Persistence should not be confused with stubbornness. Knowing when one must change course is the mark of a hi-MQ person. The next step after considering a new viewpoint is

to change your existing viewpoint if the new one is better —
even if you have held the existing viewpoint for a long time.
This is an important indicator of meta intelligence rather than
intelligence, for we all know hi-IQ individuals who can never
admit they were wrong.

Intellectual flexibility requires a certain amount of
intellectual humility. This is humility in the commendatory
sense as a check against vanity and egocentrism. Intellectual
humility is being able to accept that you might be wrong about
beliefs and assumptions you hold. Nobody demonstrated this
better than Marcus Aurelius.

As emperor of Rome at the height of its power (AD 161-
180), Aurelius was the most powerful person on earth. He
could have had or done anything he wanted, yet he was
determined to stay grounded and not let absolute power
corrupt him as it had many of his predecessors. To this end,
he regularly wrote down his thoughts and observations, of
which the collection came to be known as *The Meditations.*
This introspective work is essentially Aurelius' journal of self-
reflection. It contains brilliant insights such as the following:

If anyone can refute me, show me I'm making a mistake
or looking at things from the wrong perspective, I'll
gladly change.

It's the truth I'm after and the truth never harmed anyone.

What harms us is to persist in self-deceit and ignorance.

Eastern philosophers have always championed the virtue of being flexible as is beautifully illustrated in this passage by the great Chinese philosopher, Lao Tzu...

Men are born soft and supple;
Dead, they are stiff and hard.
Plants are born tender and pliant;
Dead, they are brittle and dry.
Thus, whoever is stiff and inflexible is a disciple of death.
Whoever is soft and yielding is a disciple of life.
The hard and stiff will be broken.
The soft and supple will prevail.

INDEPENDENT

"Most people don't know why they're doing what they're doing. They imitate others, go with the flow, and follow paths without making their own."

-Derek Sivers

Meta thinkers are open and flexible, but they are not afraid to think independently and do things differently when called for. They do not suffer from the 'herd mentality'. If after careful deliberation, they believe that their way of doing something is correct, they will follow that method – regardless of what other people might think. They trust their own judgement and are not swayed by authority, social norms, or peer pressure. They know they think and act differently and that is fine with them. Not only that but they also know they *must* think and do things differently from the herd in order to stand out and achieve something truly remarkable.

"You have to be odd to be number 1."

-Dr. Seuss

The fact of the matter is that our world wouldn't be the same were it not for the great independent thinkers throughout history who went against the prevailing dogma of the day. For example, imagine that before Copernicus and Galileo, people thought the sun revolved around the earth. Galileo was placed under house arrest until death for espousing the opposite view.

In modern times we have figures like the late great tech visionary, Steve Jobs, whose inventions such as the Apple computer, smart phone, iPad, etc. have transformed society. Jobs was known for his independent attitude as illustrated in the following eloquent passage…

Don't be trapped by dogma, which is living the result of other people's thinking. Don't let the noise of other's opinion drown your own inner voice. And most important, have the courage to follow your heart and intuition, they somehow already know what you truly want to become. Everything else is secondary.

Jobs was a trailblazer in many areas – even fashion. While other CEOs had expensive wardrobes of 3-piece suits, Jobs would wear the same black turtleneck and jeans every day. He did this so he wouldn't waste time thinking about what clothes to wear that day. Fellow tech tycoon and visionary, Mark Zuckerberg, followed in his footsteps and wears the same jeans, grey t-shirt and hoodie every day.

Another example of this maverick attitude is provided by business mogul Mark Cuban – one of the stars of the hit reality TV show, *Shark Tank.* (incidentally, Cuban's blog is fittingly called *Blog Maverick*). He recounts how at one of his first jobs selling PC software, he wanted to close a sale, but his boss told him not to. He could see no downside to closing, so he went ahead and closed anyway. He was promptly fired despite having acted in everybody's best interests. This prompted him to start his own business and the rest is history.

*

If everyone agrees with you,

then you are not being innovative enough.

*

Chapter 10:

Meta Resources

———

——

—

"What you make of life is up to you. You have all the tools and resources you need – what you do with them is up to you."

-John C. Maxwell

Perhaps the most overlooked aspect of personal development is the resource base that one should keep at their disposal in order to improve. Successful people know that resources provide the leverage to accumulate wealth and accomplish great things.

Unfortunately, too many people squander or do not recognize all the resources available to them.

There are two broad areas of resources: people and tools. In the same way that you need good people and tools to build your house, you need good people and tools to build your life.

PEOPLE

———

—

Valuable people resources include those that can provide you with financial or political capital to help you get things done.

Other people resources that are valuable are those that can provide you with knowledge and inspirational support to help you achieve your goals. These include…

- Mentors
- Coaches
- Experts
- Role models
- Online forums
- Meet up groups
- Mastermind groups

The Mastermind Group:

A mastermind is a peer to peer mentoring concept coined by Napoleon Hill and popularized in his classic books *Law of Success* and *Think and Grow Rich*. Hill was one of the first people to study the attributes of successful people.

A mastermind allows you to surround yourself with other knowledgeable and success-minded people who can help you succeed. You in turn can help others succeed depending on your area of expertise. You explore new ideas and ways of thinking as well as new ways of doing things.

"Surround yourself with positive people who believe in your dreams, encourage your ideas, support your ambitions, and bring out the best in you."

-Roy Bennett

A mastermind lets their members share resources. Each member's networks are also expanded exponentially. In other words, a mastermind group exposes you to the Skills, Habits, Attitudes, Resources, & Knowledge of other successful meta intelligent individuals a.k.a. SHARKS.

"A smart man makes a mistake, learns from it, and never makes that mistake again. But a wise man finds a smart man and learns from him how to avoid the mistake altogether."

-Roy H. Williams

Tools

———

—

One important tool is of course money. Another is information. Other useful tools are technological products such as the internet, computers, and smart phones, as well as the software and apps that run on them. There are so many terrific online resources – it's a crime not to make use of them.

Wealthy and successful people know how to leverage whatever resources they have in order to create new resources. Jeff Bezos and Mark Zuckerberg got investors to buy into their vision and they each used the internet to create Amazon & Facebook, respectively.

COGNITIVE TOOLS

———

—

Besides physical tools and e-tools, there are also cognitive tools that meta thinkers assemble (or mental models / apps etc.). You should always be looking to add new tools to your cognitive toolbox. Creating your own tools is a great cognitive exercise and it makes those tools more meaningful. For example, as you've already seen, I like to create my own tools with mnemonic acronyms like SMARTER, ME & I, MAD, SHARK, etc.

Bilateral thinking

I also created other tools such as my *bilateral thinking* tool. In bilateral thinking, I simultaneously approach a problem from two opposite sides. For example, when writing this book, I adopted a simultaneous *top-down* & *bottom-up* approach - thinking of the overall structure and details at the same time. Bilateral thinking ensures I have a balanced overall perspective of the issue at hand.

I use my bilateral thinking approach with many dualities.

e.g.

I like to innovate by simultaneously *deconstructing* and *reconstructing* things.

When I *learn* a subject, I simultaneously think of how I would *teach* that subject.

I *answer* at the same time I *question*, and I *practice* while I *study*.

The opposite of bilateral thinking is *unilateral thinking*. The dictionary.com definition of unilateral is "confined to only one side". So, unilateral thinking would be thinking that is confined to only one side (of an issue e.g.) – ignoring the other side.

The use of the word *confined* in this definition is very apropos because it connotes something negative, as in your ability to think freely is being restricted – which it is! Unilateral thinking can be unnecessarily self-limiting, yet it is quite common. I think part of the problem is that people seem to have a penchant for creating *false dichotomies* for themselves.

A true dichotomy is a division into two mutually exclusive parts. With a false dichotomy, the two parts are not mutually exclusive i.e. an individual can adopt both (styles, approaches, techniques etc.), yet people choose only one method nore the less. Not only are the parts not mutually exclusive, they complement each other, often in a yin/yang kind of way. Thus, I am perplexed as to why people choose only one approach or technique when having both would be much more beneficial.

Some false dichotomies include …

- Goals vs systems (or process / methods / habits etc.)

This false dichotomy is particularly curious since most definitions of systems will tell you that systems are collections of inter-related components organized to accomplish a goal. Goals and systems go hand in hand. A goal without a plan is like deciding on a destination without having a clue as to how to get there. Likewise, setting sail without a destination will leave you adrift. This book can be regarded as a system for the goal of improving oneself!

- Emotional vs rational

I have emphasized in this book that you can have emotional intelligence as well as meta intelligence. You can also be intuitive as well as logical.

- Divergence vs convergence

Divergent thinking looks for many different solutions; convergent thinking looks for one optimal solution. One can and should think divergently as well as convergently.

- Big picture vs details

Systems thinkers like Bill Gates and Steve Jobs were adept at effortlessly *zooming in & out* (back and forth between the components & system).

• Expert vs generalist

An expert has deep specialized knowledge in one specific field whereas a generalist has broad diverse knowledge in many fields. However, it's possible to be both and in fact many meta intelligent people are. They are *expert-generalists* – a term coined by Orit Gadiesh. Expert-generalists have both deep and broad knowledge, but more importantly …

This diverse knowledge base allows expert-generalists to draw insights on fundamental and interdisciplinary principles and apply these insights to solve problems within their core specialty.

-guidetopurposefulsuccess.com

Knowledge in one discipline can also be adapted in another discipline to create something new and interesting, like when Steve Jobs used his knowledge of calligraphy to create computer fonts at Apple.

Charlie Munger and Elon Musk are other examples of expert-generalists.

In general, when presented with a choice amongst two options, the meta intelligent person always asks, "Is it possible to have both?".

"Think left and think right."

-Dr. Seuss

—

"There is no doubt that creativity is the most important human resource of all. Without creativity, there would be no progress, and we would be forever repeating the same patterns."

-Edward de Bono

The following are some of the cognitive tools I like to use when engaged in creative problem solving or innovating.

- Divergent thinking
- Lateral thinking
- First principles thinking
- Incubation

"Imagination is more important than knowledge."

- Einstein

DIVERGENT THINKING

Divergent thinking is a method used to generate ideas by exploring several solutions in a free-flowing, non-linear manner. Being able to quickly generate many ideas / solutions pertaining to a problem is a mark of high MQ.

The concept of divergent vs. convergent thinking was formulated by psychologist J.P. Guilford in 1956, although he was undoubtedly influenced by Alex Osborn's very influential book on creative ideation, *Applied Imagination*, a couple of years earlier where Osborn introduced the technique of brainstorming (Osborn, 1953). Divergent thinking can be regarded as *individual brainstorming*. Divergent thinking is important in cognitive science because it is a widely used measure of creativity.

The concept of divergent thinking also laid the groundwork for famous variants like *lateral thinking* and its close cousn *outside the box thinking*. What cognitive approaches such as these have in common is that they recognize that there is a conventional way of thinking which most people follow, but then there are unconventional, new ways of thinking, solving problems, doing things that require a different mindset and that often lead to better solutions or ideas. And this is the essence of meta intelligence.

A classic test of creative problem solving is the *candle problem* (Duncker, 1945) where participants are given a candle, a book of matches, and a box of tacks and are required to attach the candle to a wall so that none of the wax will drip on the floor or table.

People who can think divergently will more readily find the solution: use the tack box as a candle holder and tack it to the wall. However, those who are predominantly convergent thinkers may fall victim to *functional fixedness* (the tendency to see only the intended use for something) and consequently struggle to solve the problem.

SOLUTION TO THE CANDLE PROBLEM

*"Logic will take you from A to B.
Imagination will take you everywhere."*

- Einstein

LATERAL THINKING

Latera thinking refers to solving problems using an indirect and creative approach. It typically involves viewing the problem in new ways.

Lateral thinking is just one of many great thinking techniques promulgated by meta thinker, Edward de Bono. The traditional thinking approach to problem solving can be described as *vertical thinking*, i.e. it follows a logical step by step (sequential) straight path (linear) from problem to solution. De Bono formulated the concept of lateral thinking as an alternative approach to this straightforward way of problem solving and idea origination. Lateral thinking often arrives at unexpected solutions and ideas by viewing a problem from different angles, reconceptualizing the problem, and applying non-sequential thinking.

i.pinimg.com

De Bono gives the story of the *Black Pebble* as an example (De Bono, 2014). In the story, a merchant, who is the father of a beautiful young daughter, owes money to an ogrish old lender. The lender offers the merchant the following proposition: he will put two pebbles in a sack; one is black, the other white. If the merchant's daughter picks the white pebble, the debt will be forgiven; if she picks the black pebble, the debt will be forgiven but she will be betrothed to the lender. The merchant reluctantly agrees, else he will go to jail as he is unable to repay the lender. But the unscrupulous lender picks up two black pebbles from the path and puts them in the bag.

The daughter happens to witness the sleight of hand; but what should she do? If she picks a pebble, she will be forced to marry the lender, but if she challenges the lender, her father will go to jail. Fortunately, the daughter is a lateral and meta thinker, so she picks a pebble but proceeds to quickly drop it among the other pebbles on the path. Since the remaining pebble is black, it must be assumed that she had picked the white one.

> In this way, by using lateral thinking, the girl changes what seems like an impossible situation into an extremely advantageous one. …

> Lateral thinking is easiest to appreciate when it is seen in action as in the pebble story. Everyone has come across the sort of problem that seems impossible to solve until suddenly a surprisingly simple solution is revealed. Once it has been thought of, the solution is so obvious that one cannot understand why it was ever so difficult to find. This sort of problem may indeed be difficult to solve so long as vertical thinking is used.

> (De Bono, 2014)

Thinking about the candle problem in this lateral manner will lead to thinking about the tack box in a different way and generating the solution.

FIRST PRINCIPLES THINKING

The concept of first principles has its roots in ancient philosophy. Aristotle taught that everything we attempt to understand should be broken down into elements that are known to be true, and that we should then build from those elements.

Elon Musk has made this concept popular in recent times. Musk is an extreme case of the autodidact polymath, having even taught himself rocket science! Musk wanted to get into the aerospace industry but he found the cost of buying a rocket to be prohibitively high; so, he used first principles thinking and broke down a rocket into its material constituents and realized he could buy the raw materials very cheaply and then assemble them into rockets himself. And that is how Space X was born. He used the same approach for battery packs.

Going back to our candle problem, we could solve it by deconstructing the given objects and then reconstructing them to meet the requirements of the solution. The box of tacks would be deconstructed into (1) the tacks and (2) a box that can be used to hold something – in this case a candle.

INCUBATION

Incubation is defined as a process
of **unconscious** recombination of **thought** elements that were
stimulated through **conscious** work at one point in time,
resulting in novel **ideas** at some later point in time.

(Seabrook & Dienes, 2003)

Or in more layperson's terms…

The experience of leaving a problem for a period of time and then finding that the difficulty evaporates on returning to the problem, or, even more striking, that the solution 'comes out of the blue' when thinking about something else…

-Wikipedia/Incubation

Researchers believe there is substantial cognitive activity that takes place below the conscious surface. This activity helps to coalesce and make sense of our thoughts floating on the surface. This is why taking frequent breaks from strenuous mental work is a good strategy.

Many breakthroughs have come during periods of relaxation. The most celebrated example of incubation is undoubtedly Archimedes' 'bathtub eureka moment'. Archimedes had been struggling to find a way to measure the volume of irregular objects. He put the problem aside and decided to take a bath. While getting into the tub, he noticed that his body was displacing water. At that moment, he suddenly realized that the volume of water displaced by an object was equal to the volume of the object. The gifted Greek was so excited that he ran naked through the streets of Syracuse shouting "Eureka! (Greek for 'I found it'), Eureka!".

Perhaps inspired by Archimedes, Elon Musk, when asked what the most productive part of his day was, answered: "My morning shower, that's when I get most of my ideas."

I have often used incubation to tackle stubborn problems. I find it truly remarkable how effective letting your nonconscious mind work on a problem can be. What is even more remarkable is that your nonconscious mind can work on a problem in your dreams! Researchers like Harvard psychologist, Deirdre Barrett, have studied this phenomenon in artists and scientists, reporting dramatic anecdotes of ingenious ideas originating in dreams. Barrett advises success minded people to always keep a notepad by their bed for those moments of nocturnal inspiration. (Barrett, 2001)

For example, the German chemist, Kekule had been struggling to find the molecular structure of benzene. Then one night he dreamt of a snake biting its tail, and he realized right away that this was the solution – the benzene molecule was a ring! This breakthrough was tremendously important for our understanding of aromatic compounds. And to think that it was the result of a dream!

*"A problem difficult at night is resolved in the
morning after the committee of sleep has worked on
it."*

- John Steinbeck

"Never go to sleep without a request to your subconscious."

- Thomas Edison

=-=-=

These are but a few of the many creative thinking tools available. Learning about these and other creativity tools is time well spent. When solving problems, you will be able to draw upon one or more of these tools. For example, revisit Duncker's *candle problem* and see if you can come up with alternative solutions (I can think of a couple of others).

Another famous Duncker problem is the *radiation problem* (Duncker, 1945) where you are a doctor charged with destroying a patient's inoperable stomach tumor using rays. The challenge is that high intensity rays will destroy the tumor, but they will also destroy healthy tissue while low intensity rays will destroy neither. How can you destroy the tumor without killing the patient? Try to come up with more than one solution.

CHAPTER 11:

META KNOWLEDGE

Epistemologists have identified various types and subtypes of knowledge but the one that is of interest to us for building our meta shark is *metacognitive knowledge*. Metacognitive knowledge refers to what individuals know about themselves and others as cognitive processors i.e. as learners and thinkers.

Metacognitive knowledge includes:

1. *Declarative knowledge*: refers to knowledge about oneself as a learner and about what factors can influence one's performance. Declarative knowledge can also be referred to as "world knowledge".

2. *Procedural knowledge*: refers to knowledge about doing things. This type of knowledge is displayed as heuristics and strategies. A high degree of procedural knowledge can allow individuals to perform tasks more automatically. This is achieved through a large variety of strategies that can be accessed more efficiently.
3. *Conditional knowledge*: refers to knowing when and why to use declarative and procedural knowledge. It allows learners to allocate their resources when using strategies. This in turn allows the strategies to become more effective.

-wikipedia

Having a high degree of metacognitive knowledge helps one to identify obstacles to learning and to change strategies in order to overcome those obstacles. I would contend that metacognitive knowledge is one of the factors that most separates the meta intelligent from others. When it comes to IQ and learning, metacognition can be the *great equalizer.* (Swanson, 1990)   found that metacognitive knowledge can compensate for IQ and lack of prior knowledge when comparing problem solving in fifth and sixth grade students. High metacognition students used fewer strategies, but solved problems more effectively than low metacognition students, regardless of IQ or prior knowledge.

THE COMPUTER ANALOGY

———

—

The use of the computer as a model for how the human mind handles information is known as the computer analogy. The human mind is much more complex than a computer but, nonetheless, both are essentially information processing systems. Information processing theory in psychology is based on this observation.

I find the computer analogy useful for conceptualizing meta intelligence as well. A computer has the following components which correspond to components of the mind…

1. A memory component where data can be stored.

This corresponds to our own memory. MQ makes use of metacognitive declarative knowledge stored there.

2. Processes and software programs that input, process, & output information.

This corresponds to our mindware. MQ uses our mindware's procedural knowledge such as systems, strategies, processes, etc. that we assemble over time.

3. An operating system that manages these processes and software.

This corresponds to our executive functions. MQ acts as a controller, using conditional knowledge to regulate our declarative and procedural knowledge.

We all make use of these of these components; however, it is a premise of this book that they are more fully developed in meta intelligent individuals.

At first glance, the computer analogy may just seem like a simple model of the brain, but it has far-reaching philosophical and practical implications in many areas such as learning and thinking.

To begin with, if we accept the computer analogy, then we must also accept the notion that we can improve our intelligence and overall cognitive functioning by improving the components of the personal computer that resides inside our heads – especially our software and operating system. And this is what MQ is all about.

The computer analogy has implications for how we view behaviour as well. In the same way that a computer's software processes information to produce output, so too do our mental programs act on our stored knowledge files to produce our behaviour. Better programs and knowledge result in better behaviour.

IGNORANCE AND META IGNORANCE

———

—

"Real knowledge is to know the extent of one's ignorance."
-Confucius

We can also categorize knowledge as Donald Rumsfeld did in terms of knowns and unknowns when he made the following famous / infamous statement to justify going into Iraq.

"As we know, there are known knowns; ... things we know we know. We also know there are known unknowns, i.e. we know there are some things we do not know. But there are also **unknown unknowns** — the ones we don't know we don't know."

-Donald Rumsfeld

But as many have cheekily pointed out, he omitted a fourth possibility: refusing to believe what is known. This gives us the following *ignorance matrix*…

	Comprehend	Not Comprehend
Aware	Known Knowns	Known Unknowns
Not Aware	Unknown Knowns	Unknown Unknowns

The Ignorance Matrix

Known Knowns

The known knowns quadrant reflects conscious knowledge: awareness of what we know i.e. things we know we have learnt and understand.

One interesting difference between meta thinkers and the average person is that meta thinkers are aware that what they know is relatively miniscule compared to what they don't know. Many people tend to over-estimate what they know and under-estimate what they don't know. The ability to accurately gage one's knowledge is an important aspect of meta intelligence (e.g. Warren Buffett's *circle of competence* mental model).

> *"The more our knowledge*
> *increases, the more our ignorance*
> *unfolds"*
>
> -John F. Kennedy

Known Unknowns

This quadrant reflects our conscious ignorance: we know there are things we haven't learnt i.e. we are aware of the things we don't understand.

Because there are so many unknowns, meta thinkers determine which are worth learning about and which are best to ignore. You would typically prioritize learning the things that will be the most useful to you in achieving your goals. Meta intelligent people are skilled at quickly identifying what needs to be learned to accomplish a task or goal.

*"To know that we know what we know, and to know that we
do not know what we do not know - that is true knowledge"*

-Copernicus

Unknown Knowns

This quadrant reflects our nonconscious knowledge: we have learnt things, but we have repressed or temporarily forgotten that knowledge. This might happen when we have painful memories or knowledge that does not coincide with our beliefs.

Unknown Unknowns

*"The fool doth think he is wise, but the
wise man knows himself to be a fool"*

-Shakespeare

Unknown unknowns reflect our true ignorance: blind spots in life that we do not even know exist. Ignorance of one's ignorance is referred to as *meta ignorance*. Studies have repeatedly shown that individuals of lower intellectual ability vastly overestimate their intellectual capabilities. This finding shouldn't be surprising, for as comedian John Cleese puts it …

"If you're very stupid, how can you possibly realize that you're very, very stupid? You'd have to be relatively intelligent to realize how stupid you are."

Fascinated by the profound incompetence of some of 'America's dumbest criminals', psychologist David Dunning along with his grad student Justin Kruger studied meta ignorance in individuals.

David Dunning wrote about his observations that people with substantial, measurable deficits in their knowledge or expertise lack the ability to recognize those deficits and, therefore, despite potentially making error after error, tend to think they are performing competently when they are not: "In short, those who are incompetent, for lack of a better term, should have little insight into their incompetence".

-Wikipedia/ Dunning-Kruger effect

This observation has famously come to be known as the Dunning–Kruger effect. Everybody knows of someone who believes they excel at something but in reality, they are horribly incompetent at it. They are completely oblivious as to their ignorance – in other words they are meta ignorant. But as Dunning cautioned, don't feel too smug, because we are all 'confident idiots' to some extent.

"Ignorance more frequently begets confidence than does knowledge."

-Charles Darwin

CHAPTER 12:
MASTERING COGNITIVE SOCIAL AWARENESS

"Let it be your constant method to look into the design of people's actions, and see what they would be at, as often as it is practicable; and to make this custom the more significant, practice it first upon yourself."

-Marcus Aurelius

n previous chapters, I focused on cognitive self-awareness. In this chapter, I will discuss cognitive social awareness. Once again, I insert the *cognitive* qualifier to distinguish it from *emotional* social awareness.

If we define cognitive self-awareness as being aware of what and how we think as well as why we think and do the thing we do, then cognitive social awareness can be defined as being aware of what and how others think as well as why they think and do the things they do. This entails trying to understand the mindsets, inclinations, and rationale of others – especially as they pertain to us.

> "The master said, even when walking in a party of
> no more than three, I can always be certain of
> learning from those I am with. There will be good
> qualities that I can select for imitation and bad ones
> that will teach me what requires correction in
> myself."
>
> -Confucius

WHY WE SHOULD MASTER SOCIAL META

INTELLIGENCE

———

—

There may be many reasons for mastering our cognitive social awareness. For example:

- We do not want to be unduly influenced or manipulated by others.
- We want to use our knowledge of others' inclinations to predict their behaviour and favourably adjust our own behaviour in response. This is especially true the more their behaviour impacts us.
- We want to expand our social network.
- We want to associate with people who can help us and not associate with people who can harm us.
- We want to learn from others.
- We need to interact effectively with the different types of people we may come across.
- We want our relationships to flourish.

"The quality of your life is the quality of your relationships."

-Tony Robbins

BUILDING YOUR SOCIAL SHARK

———

—

In a previous chapter, I introduced the concept of the meta shark as part of our cognitive self-awareness development. When developing your cognitive social awareness, you will be building a social shark. A social shark is an example of a 'child' shark. A child shark inherits the properties of its parent (in this case the meta shark) and adds new ones that deal with a specific context – in this case, the social context.

Let's look at a possible social shark…

SKILLS

Empathy

Empathy is the cornerstone of social awareness and the most valuable social skill one can have.

There are two major types of empathy…

1. Emotional (heart)

Emotional empathy is also referred to as affective empathy and is characterized by *emotional contagion* i.e. feeling others' emotions. In this type of empathy, emotions are shared vicariously.

2. Cognitive (mind)

Cognitive empathy is also referred to as *perspective-taking* because you mentally put yourself in someone else's shoes to see things from their perspective. There are two shoes…

- Assessing / inferring what others are feeling (e.g. emotions)

This is different from emotional empathy because it involves <u>reasoning</u> about others' emotions.

- Assessing / inferring what others are thinking (e.g. desires, beliefs, intentions, knowledge)

Emotional empathy is associated with EQ, while cognitive empathy is what I associate with MQ. No less an authority on social skills than Dale Carnegie regarded cognitive empathy as being paramount for success. The following is an excerpt from his highly influential book, *How to Win Friends and Influence People* (Carnegie, 1936) …

"If out of reading this book, you get just one thing – an increased tendency to think always in terms of other people's point of view and see things from their angle…it may easily prove to be one of the building blocks of your career."

And no less an authority on achieving success than Henry Ford also regarded cognitive empathy as indispensable for success…

"If there is any one secret of success, it lies in the ability to get the other person's point of view and see things from that person's angle as well as from your own."

Cognitive empathy uses knowledge and logical reasoning to deduce and predict another person's mental state and consequent behaviour. Cognitive empathy is indispensable for improving social interactions and relationships. It is also indispensable in other contexts as well, e.g. product designers and marketers have always known the value of "getting inside their customers' heads".

An important subtype of cognitive empathy is *strategic empathy* i.e. "the strategic use of perspective-taking to achieve a certain objective". This type of empathy is prevalent in business and politics. Unfortunately, scammers, psychopaths, and other manipulative types who lack emotional empathy are often adept at strategic empathy. This is all the more reason why we should always ask ourselves: "what's in it for them?".

Cognitive empathy is a crucial skill that should constantly be honed. When you do practice cognitive empathy, be mindful of your biases and be careful not to *project* your mental state onto others.

People skills

It goes without saying that having effective people skills would go a long way in dealing with people. Fortunately, there is no shortage of literature on this subject. Dale Carnegie's *How to Win Friends and Influence People* is as good now as it was then.

Critical thinking skills in human interactions

"When dealing with people, remember you are not dealing with creatures of logic, but with creatures bristling with prejudice and motivated by pride and vanity."

-Dale Carnegie

Human interactions are rife with emotional and cognitive biases as well as errors of logic which often result in ineffective or even dysfunctional relations.

Eliminating thinking errors in the social domain will result in more satisfactory relations. To this end we must once again rely on SMARTER thinking and apply it to social situations. For example, rational thinking is a great tool for *bias correction,* and being systems-minded and thinking in second order terms will prevent a lot of unfortunate *unintended consequences.*

HABITS

- Interact with many people / network

There are two types of networks: open and closed. In a closed network, everyone thinks like you. In an open network, people have different ways of thinking. Open networks are crucial for learning about different perspectives and bursting your ideological bubble (see appendix of mental models).

"Through our connections with unique people, we are able to gain a true understanding of the world around us."

-Peter Senge

- Pay attention to your inner circle.

"One wrong person in your circle can destroy your future. It's that important."

-Terry Crews

*

The people you spend the most time with, influence you the most.

*

- Associate with people who have hi EQ & MQ

"Find a group of people who challenge and inspire you, spend a lot of time with them, and it will change your life."

-Amy Poehler

- Associate with successful people

"Keep away from those who try to belittle your ambitions. Small people always do that but the really great make you believe you can become great too."

-Mark Twain

- Learn from role models

"A wise man ought always to follow the paths beaten by great men, and to imitate those who have been supreme, so that if his ability does not equal theirs, at least it will savour of it."

-Machiavelli

- Learn from mentors

"Associate with people who are likely to improve you."

-Seneca

The list of famous successful people who had great mentors is endless. For example,

Steve Jobs mentored Mark Zuckerberg
Jim Rohn mentored Tony Robbins
Maya Angelou mentored Oprah Winfrey
W. Clement Stone mentored Jack Canfield

"If you want to achieve superlative success, you must apprentice to a master."

-Robert Allen

- Learn from anyone and everyone you meet

> *"I never met a man so ignorant that I couldn't learn something from him."*
>
> -Galileo

- Seek feedback (including criticism)

> *"We all need people who will give us feedback. That's how we improve."*
>
> -Bill Gates

- Don't be shy to seek help when needed

> *"Ask, and you shall succeed!"*
>
> -M. R. Kopmeyer

Former U.S. president Barack Obama puts it well…

> *"Don't be afraid to ask for help when you need it. I do that every day. Asking for help isn't a sign of weakness, it's a sign of strength.*

It shows you have the courage to admit when you don't know something, and to learn something new."

If the former president of the United States has the humility to ask for help, you should too.

"One of the biggest defects in life is the inability to ask for help."

-Robert Kiyosaki

- People-watch

You can people-watch anywhere but one of my favorite pass-times is sitting at a cafe and observing people as I sip my latte. I watch the baristas & observe how they do their job. I also watch how the customers behave.

I like to observe what people do and evaluate how well they do it. For example, when at a store or restaurant, I observe and evaluate the choices made by the ownership/management and how I could improve upon them.

- Observe office politics

This can be entertaining as well as instructive.

- Play games where you must predict how other players will behave e.g. poker, role playing games

- Watch movies.

Watching movies is like *virtual people-watching*.

Don't just watch movies passively, watch them meta intelligently – carefully analyzing and evaluating the characters and the interpersonal dynamics.

Detective movies are a good choice since detectives usually have a high degree of meta intelligence. The cat and mouse games between detective and villain are both fascinating and instructive to watch e.g. Sherlock Holmes, Columbo.

Movies are also good because they help you to understand different kinds of people – good and bad, healthy and unhealthy. For example, if you see the movie *Gaslight,* you will be much more likely to recognize a gaslighting narcissist and spare yourself a lot of grief.

- Read novels
  Same idea as watching movies.

- Read autobiographies, biographies

ATTITUDES

- It all starts with being curious about how other people think and wanting to understand their beliefs, desires, objectives, motives, etc.

- Being open towards others will help you understand them better

RESOURCES

- Internet
- Social media
- The people resources described in the meta shark are important here as well e.g. a mentor at work can help you navigate the politics and culture of a corporation.

*"Surround yourself only with
people who are going to lift you
higher."*

-Oprah Winfrey

KNOWLEDGE

*"Know your enemy and know yourself,
then you need not fear the result of a hundred battles."*

-Sun Tzu

In the first part of this book we were concerned with knowledge of the self; now we will concern ourselves with knowledge of others. We want to know such things as a person's disposition, personality, and character traits. We also may want to know what a person's thoughts, attitudes, and beliefs are.

Knowledge of psychology and sociology is valuable for understanding human tendencies. Also valuable are first-hand accounts from military, political, & business leaders such as Sun Tzu (*The Art of War*), Marcus Aurelius (*Meditations*), Machiavelli (*The Prince*), & Charlie Munger (*Poor Charlie's Almanac*).

"We are much beholden to Machiavelli and others that write what men do, and not what they ought to do."

-Francis Bacon

THE PERSPECTIVE PROBLEM

Different people may all be looking at the same thing, yet they will all view it differently. I refer to this situation as the *perspective problem* and it is beautifully illustrated by the parable of the blind men and the elephant…

A long time ago, a group of blind men heard that there was a strange animal in their village. They wished to know what this animal was, so they went to investigate. The first blind man, whose hand landed on the trunk, said "This creature is like a snake". For another one whose hand reached its ear, it seemed kind of like a fan. Another person, whose hand was upon its leg, said "This animal is like a tree-trunk". The blind man who placed his hand upon its side said, "the animal is like a wall". Another who felt its tail, described it as a rope. The last felt its tusk, stating the animal is like a spear.

And so, despite the fact they were touching the same animal, the blind men disagreed on what it was because they were focused on different parts of it. Not only did they disagree but they argued incessantly, and each accused the others of being mad.

The solution to the perspective problem is what I refer to as *perspective-switching*: a perspective-taking variant where you switch your perspective with someone else's in order to get a more complete picture of a situation and be better able to resolve it. Your goal is to be able to use their thinking strategies and mental models which would ordinarily reside outside your mindware space. We all have different perspectives because we are all specialized components of social systems. Consequently, our knowledge and mental models are specialized.

Charlie Munger was aware of this. In his 1995 speech (the psychology of human misjudgement) he states…

"Well, the first rule is that you've got to have multiple models — because if you just have one or two that you're using, the nature of human psychology is such that you'll torture reality so that it fits your models, or at least you'll think it does. You become the equivalent of a chiropractor who, of course, is the great boob in medicine. It's like the old saying, "to the man with only a hammer, every problem looks like a nail." And of course, that's the way the chiropractor goes about practicing medicine.

But that's a perfectly disastrous way to think and a perfectly disastrous way to operate in the world.

So, you've got to have multiple models. And the models have to come from multiple disciplines — because all the wisdom of the world is not to be found in one little academic department. That's why poetry professors, by and large, are so unwise in a worldly sense. They don't have enough models in their heads. So, you've got to have models across a fair array of disciplines."

And then, Farnam Street picked up the torch…

Most of us, however, are specialists. Instead of a latticework of mental models, we have a few from our discipline. Each specialist sees something different. By default, a typical Engineer will think in systems. A psychologist will think in terms of incentives. A biologist will think in terms of evolution. By putting these disciplines together in our head, we can walk around a problem in a three-dimensional way. If we're only looking at the problem one way, we've got a blind spot. And blind spots can kill you.

Here's another way to think about it. When a botanist looks at a forest they may focus on the ecosystem; an environmentalist sees the impact of climate change; a forestry engineer, the state of the tree growth; a businessperson, the value of the land. None are wrong, but neither are any of them able to describe the full scope of the forest. Sharing knowledge, or learning the basics of the other disciplines, would lead to a

Our perspectives are also different and limited because of differences in our personalities and mindsets. So, it is beneficial to know our own personalities and mindsets and how they differ from those of others. We can then approach situations from different psychological perspectives. Our psychological perspectives are shaped to a large extent by our individual demographic backgrounds.

e.g.

- Age
- Gender
- Race
- Marital status
- Number of children (if any)
- Occupation
- Annual income
- Education level
- Living status (homeowner or renter)
- Political affiliation
- Religious affiliation
- Nationality
- Disabilities (if any)
- Social class (lower, middle, or upper-class)

So, it is often useful when trying to understand a societal problem to switch between different demographic / cultural perspectives.

*"If you're only thinking about yourself,
you can't see the whole picture."*

-Chris Hadfield

———

—

"To understand the true quality of people, you must look into their minds, and examine their pursuits and aversions."

-Marcus Aurelius

PERCEPTIONS

The process of forming impressions and inferences about other people is known as *social perception*. Perceptions take place, either through observation or interaction with others.

First impressions (*primacy effect*) are important, as are final impressions (*recency effect*), for people tend to remember them more so than those in between. First impressions are crucial though, because you may not get a chance to make a second impression!

You should be aware that anytime you meet people, they will be *perceiving* you and unfortunately perception is not a perfect process. 'Don't judge a book by its cover' is a familiar idiom; however, when perceiving others, people tend to do just that. They are quick to make inferences about people based solely on their appearance.

Psychosocial Biases

Perceptions of people are prone to a slew of psychosocial biases such as the following…

Stereotyping – Attributing traits to individuals based on traits of the group they belong to.

Halo effect – Tendency for the overall impression of an individual to affect the observer's feelings and thoughts about other attributes or traits of the individual.

False-consensus effect – Tendency for people to overestimate the degree to which others share their behaviors, opinions, and attributes.

Perceptual expectancy – Tendency for people to perceive what they expect or want to perceive.

Being aware of your biases will lead to more accurate perceptions of others.

"When people rely on surface appearances and false racial stereotypes, rather than in-depth knowledge of others at the level of the heart, mind, and spirit, their ability to assess and understand people accurately is compromised."

-James A. Forbes

ATTRIBUTIONS

The knowledge we assemble about others is useful because it helps predict or explain people's behaviour. Using this knowledge to explain people's behaviour is known as *attribution*. One parameter in attribution is whether the behaviour was due to the internal disposition of the person or whether it was due to external circumstances.

Attribution Biases

Attribution is susceptible to the *fundamental attribution error* which overestimates the influence of internal vs external factors when explaining another person's behaviour. However, when explaining our own behaviour, we tend to attribute external causes (*actor-observer bias*). This is especially true when assigning blame regarding one of our own actions - we conveniently tend to place the blame on external factors. Nevertheless, when we do something successfully, we tend to attribute internal causes (*self-serving bias*).

PERSONALITY

—

*

**Your appearance can make a good first impression,
but your personality makes a lasting one.**

*

A large part of our social perceptions deals with recognizing personality traits in others. Personality refers to the characteristic way a person thinks, feels, and behaves.

Knowing others' personalities is useful because an individual's personality is relatively stable and a good predictor of future behavior. An introvert and an extrovert will behave in very different but predictable ways in a social situation for example.

Certain traits are thought to be more influential than others in the formation of an overall impression of an individual; these are called central traits. Presently, the Big Five trait theory is the dominant theory in personality research. The big five personality traits are…

- Openness (to experience)
- Conscientiousness
- Extraversion
- Agreeableness
- Neuroticism

Each of these traits represents a continuum between two extremes and most people will be a blend of both.

People who score high on openness are creative and curious, and open to trying new things. People who score low are unimaginative and resistant to change.

People who rank high in conscientiousness have good impulse control and goal-directed behaviours. They are determined to finish important tasks right away. People who rank low fail to complete necessary or assigned tasks.

People who are high in extraversion, enjoy meeting new people and have a large social circle. Introverts, on the other hand, have a lower level of social engagement and often prefer time alone.

People high in agreeableness exhibit prosocial behaviours such as altruism and cooperation while those low in this dimension are competitive or even manipulative.

People high in neuroticism are chronic worriers and are constantly stressed and anxious. People who rank low are very resilient and emotionally stable.

A point to bear in mind is that individuals can demonstrate characteristics contrary to their personality type depending on circumstances. For example, an introvert may enter social situations and be quite adept at it if required to do so. An extrovert may successfully work alone if necessary. I would posit that this chameleon-like ability to adapt their personality type is particularly prevalent in meta intelligent individuals.

———

—

There are many examples of social MQ at work on the silver screen. The following are examples of meta intelligent movie characters who demonstrated excellent social perception and empathic skills.

Sheriff of Nottingham: 'The Adventures of Robin Hood'

The sheriff devises the famous clever trap to capture Robin by announcing an archery tournament with the prize to be presented by Lady Marian. Robin can't resist taking part in the tournament and is taken prisoner.

The ploy succeeds because the sheriff correctly reasons that Robin's pride will cause him to let down his guard in order to prove he's the best archer in the land. The sheriff also perceives that Robin has taken a liking to Marian and will want to see her again.

Ma Jarrett: 'White Heat'

In *White Heat*, James Cagney plays Cody Jarrett, the violent and volatile leader of the Jarrett criminal gang. In stark contrast to her mercurial son, Ma Jarrett is very phlegmatic. In addition to being calm and cool, she is also meta intelligently calculating.

An example of this is when Cody suffers one of his migraine episodes. His mother comforts him in his bedroom and won't let him come out until he is completely rid of his migraine and back to his normal tough self. She does this so that the other gang members won't detect any signs of weakness.

Another example is when Cody is in jail but one of the gang members, Big Ed, is having an affair with his wife. Big Ed seems to be unconcerned that Cody will exact vengeance when he gets out. Ma Jarrett reasons that Ed is not expecting Cody to get out of jail and that Ed is probably orchestrating a hit job on him while he is in prison. Ma Jarrett consequently warns Cody to be vigilant while he's in jail.

Michael Corleone: 'The Godfather I & II'

In the *Godfather* movies, Michael Corleone rises to become the Godfather and successfully lead the Corleone empire (where his brothers failed). I would argue that this was in large part because he was highly meta intelligent and there are various manifestations of this in Godfather I & II.

For example, in *The Godfather II*, he is reluctant to invest in Cuba after witnessing a rebel blow himself up. He reasons that the revolution must be a cause that the rebels deeply believe in for them to give their lives up for.

The next time you watch these classics, compare Michael's cognitive and emotional traits with those of his brothers.

John McHale: 'Die Hard'

In the iconic movie *Die Hard* there is a memorable scene where John McHale & the leader of the German terrorists, Hans, run into each other. Since Hans is unarmed, he thinks quickly and puts on an American accent pretending to be an innocent bystander. John then gives Hans a gun, so he can help him fight the terrorists. Hans promptly proceeds to shoot McHale only to discover that the gun wasn't loaded.

Many people regarded this as a hole in the plot of an otherwise perfect movie – for how could McHale possibly know that Hans was a terrorist? Yet in fact there was no hole here – McHale played it perfectly.

Firstly, he was able to control his emotions to remain calm and collected – correctly reasoning that if he displayed any apprehensiveness, he would reveal that he is unsure about who Hans really is.

Then, he quickly put himself in Hans' position (perspective taking) to determine what he would do if he were Hans. He realized there were only two possibilities – either Hans is a terrorist, or he isn't. But in either case, he will appear innocent because he is unarmed. McHale can't shoot Hans because he is not sure if he is a terrorist, so he bides his time to get a better determination. In the meantime, he lays a trap by giving him an empty pistol. Hans falls into the trap and so McHale has successfully induced Hans into revealing his true identity.

Chapter 13:

Social relationships

A social relationship can be characterized by the types of social interactions it contains. Social interactions are the processes by which we act and react to those around us.

RATIONAL INTERACTIONS

———

—

The most popular theory to explain social interactions is *social exchange theory* which is based on the concept of people as rational agents.

SOCIAL EXCHANGE THEORY

Whenever people interact in an effort to receive a reward or a return for their actions, an exchange has taken place. Exchange is a social process whereby social behavior is exchanged for some type of reward of equal or greater value. The reward can be material (a paycheck from your employer) or nonmaterial (praise from your boss).

Exchange theorists argue that behavior that is rewarded tends to be repeated; however, when the costs of an interaction outweigh the rewards, individuals are likely to end the relationship.

Proponents of exchange theory view exchange as the most basic type of social interaction. They argue that all social relations involve a give-and-take of valued resources, such as prestige or money.

Social exchange theory is based on the concept of rational choice.

Rational Choice Theory

Rational choice theory focuses on how people weigh the benefits and costs of interaction. It assumes people are rational agents that always try to maximize benefits and minimize costs.

=-=-=

However, I see some obvious problems with social exchange theory. To begin with, we have already seen that people do not always act rationally. Researchers like Kahneman (cognitive bias) and Stanovich (dysrationalia) have demonstrated this. Psychotherapists from Freud to Aaron Beck also showed how people's view of reality can be altered by subconscious forces and cognitive distortions.

Secondly, it fails to account for the many types of relationships where people do not seem to act in their best interests e.g. altruistic and toxic relationships.

=-=-=

And then there are models of social interaction that make the assumption that people are inherently good, and that they try to act accordingly. As much as I would like this to be the case, we cannot presuppose that people will act in a well-meaning manner.

"Today, I shall encounter violence, jealousy, self-seeking... All of them, the result of men not knowing what is good and what is evil."

-Marcus Aurelius

Irrational interactions

———

—

Due to the inherent problems of traditional social interaction theories, I propose a different approach to categorizing social interactions. The theory of social interaction I propose, *Fundamental Interactions Theory*, is based on two key assumptions which are in direct contrast to traditional assumptions of social interaction …

1. People are mostly irrational agents. (Irrational Agent Theory)
2. We cannot expect everyone to be good: people can be good, bad, or neutral. (Trivalent Theory of Intentions)

IRRATIONAL AGENT THEORY

This is the opposite of rational choice theory. It assumes that, for the most part, people are irrational agents that do not perform advantageous cost / benefit calculations. People often make suboptimal or just plain downright irrational choices.

There are several reasons for this.

- Humans are not machines.
- People are full of cognitive and emotional biases as well as being prone to the other types of thinking errors I outlined previously.
- They are susceptible to human temptations such as the seven deadly sins which lead them astray.
- They may have psychological problems.
- They may not have access to all the pertinent information.
- They may have cognitive control issues.
- They have cognitive load and processing limitations.
- They are limited in their ability to perform mathematical / probability calculations.

One person who recognizes our irrationality is cartoonist Scott Adams. People's irrationality is a central theme of his books and Dilbert comic strip…

"Few things are as destructive and limiting as a worldview that assumes people are mostly rational."

…

"Some famous philosophers, some scientists, and at least one cartoonist would speculate that inaccurate world views are the only kind there is."

(Adams, 2013)

*

We are essentially irrational beings,

pretending to be rational.

*

TRIVALENT THEORY of INTENTIONS: The good, bad, & indifferent

Social theorists like to assume that people are inherently good and will choose to cooperate with one another. But simple observation dictates that we cannot make this assumption. There are many reasons for why this might be the case. Differences in personalities and ideologies usually come into play, and even though individuals may belong to one society, at the same time, they also compete with one another. The result of all this is that social relationships can be complicated and far from cooperative.

High school teachers, starting out, are often given the advice that despite their best intentions, 1/3 of students will like them (& be very cooperative), 1/3 will dislike them (& potentially be uncooperative), & 1/3 will be indifferent towards them. And this is more or less the case for people in general.

Once we accept this fact, we can learn to recognize people's intentions towards us and develop strategies to deal with them.

People can have either positive, negative, or neutral feelings towards others and consequently people act either in a positive (help), negative (hurt), or neutral manner towards each other. This results in the following 3x3 matrix of dyadic social interactions which I call the *Fundamental Interactions Matrix* …

Cooperation	Altruism	Masochism
I help You	I help You	I help You
You help Me	You are neutral	You harm Me
Opportunism	**Neutrality**	**Victimism**
I am neutral	I am neutral	I am neutral
You help Me	You are neutral	You harm Me
Sadism	**Psychopathy**	**Combat**
I harm You	I harm You	I harm You
You help Me	You are neutral	You harm Me

The Fundamental Interactions Matrix

FUNDAMENTAL INTERACTIONS THEORY

Because people do not always act rationally, and people's intentions are not always restricted to beneficence, we get the nine possible types of social interactions summarized in the Fundamental Interactions Matrix. It is important to be familiar with these nine interactions because it is guaranteed that each of your social interactions will fall into one of the nine fundamental relationships:

Nine Fundamental Interpersonal Relationships

N.B. the labels I use are based on actual clinical labels but do not correspond fully with them. My main objective is to distinguish between the nine different types of social interactions.

1. **Cooperation**
   We help each other
2. **Altruism**
   I help you even though you don't help me
3. **Masochism**
   I help you but you hurt me
4. **Opportunism**
   You help me even though I don't help you
5. **Neutrality**
   We are indifferent towards each other
   (using the neutral connotation of indifferent)
6. **Victimism**
   You hurt me even though I don't hurt you

7. **Sadism**
   I hurt you even though you help me
8. **Psychopathy**
   I hurt you even though you don't hurt me
9. **Combat**
   We hurt each other

It is important to note that there are only three symmetrical relationships: cooperative, neutral, & combative. The rest are unbalanced – something other models of social relationships cannot account for but is readily observable in society.

Nine Fundamental Types of People

These fundamental relationships give rise in turn to nine fundamental psychosocial archetypes …

1. **Cooperators**
   strive for win / win interactions.
2. **Altruists**
   live to help others.
3. **Masochists**
   let others hurt them.
4. **Opportunists**
   There is nothing wrong with accepting gifts or asking for something every now and then. The problem arises when it becomes a self-seeking life strategy.
5. **Neutrals**
   are indifferent towards others.

6. **Victims**
    There are true victims and then there are pseudo victims who like to wallow in self-pity and then blame others for their misery.
7. **Sadists**
    derive pleasure in hurting others, even those who are close to them.
8. **Psychopaths**
    hurt innocent people to get what they want.
9. **Combatants**
    hurt each other.

The Deplorable Duo: Sadists & Psychopaths

The biggest difference between sadists and psychopaths is that psychopaths lack emotional empathy (though they are typically masters of strategic empathy) while sadists use their affective empathy to experience their victims' pain vicariously.

An important consideration here is that the two interacting agents need not know each other personally. For example, the reach and anonymity of the internet has given rise to a large number of trolls and scammers who target thousands of innocent people they do not know personally.

Examples

- Sociopaths
- Abusers
- Manipulators

- Machiavellians
- Narcissists
- Serial killers
- Bullies
- Swindlers
- Scammers
- Trolls

*"Don't let negative and toxic people rent space in your head.
Raise the rent and kick them out."*
*"It's amazing how quickly things can turn around when you
remove toxic people from your life."*

-Robert Tew

The Dysfunctional Duo: Masochists & (pseudo) Victims

*"Don't ask why people keep hurting you.
Ask yourself why you are allowing it to happen."*
"Stop giving love to those who don't return it."

-Robert Tew

Examples

- Doormats
- Codependents
- Self-pitiers

"How you choose to feel today should not be dependent on others."

-Anthon St. Maarten

"Poisonous people do not deserve your time. To think otherwise is masochistic."

-Tim Ferriss

The Darling Duo: Cooperators & Altruists

Cooperators and altruists undoubtedly have higher levels of empathy than other types.

Examples

- Team players

- Heroes
  e.g. Mother Teresa, Nelson Mandela, Gandhi

- Philanthropists

Some famous philanthropists include…

  - Bill Gates – Bill & Melinda Gates Foundation
  - Warren Buffett – Buffett Foundation

- Mark Zuckerberg – Chan Zuckerberg Initiative
- Jeff Bezos – Bezos Day One Fund
- Oprah Winfrey – Oprah Winfrey Charitable Foundation
- Jerry Seinfeld – GOOD+
- Will Smith – Will & Jada Smith Family Foundation
- Tony Robbins – Tony Robbins Foundation
- J.K. Rowling – Lumos
- Pitbull – SLAM
- Bono – ONE

=-=-=

Throughout your life, you will enter into many social relationships (willingly or unwillingly) and it is important to know what kind of individual you are involved with and what type of relationship you are in. As you can see from the interpersonal interaction matrix, the potential to enter a toxic relationship is high. By being aware of the nine fundamental relationships and psychosocial archetypes, you can spare yourself a lot of grief.

"We cannot dream of a Utopia in which all arrangements are ideal and everyone is flawless."

-John W. Gardner

*

Do not hurt others, and do not let others hurt you.

*

———

—

*"Stop letting people who do so little for you,
control so much of your mind, feelings, and
emotions."*

-Will Smith

A mind game can be defined as …

"a psychological tactic used to manipulate or intimidate"

-Merriam Webster

Mind games are a favorite tool of manipulative toxic people such as the *deplorable duo*, and it pays to be able to recognize them. Some common games are …

Gaslighting

Many people are familiar with this tactic because of the famous movie, Gaslight, which gives it its name.

To gaslight someone is to psychologically manipulate them into questioning their own sanity. This is typically done by the manipulator contradicting the victim's perception of reality.

Guilt-tripping

To guilt-trip someone is to induce an unjustified feeling of guilt in them. The victim is then persuaded to do something for the manipulator as a way of expunging their guilt.

Silent Treatment

To give someone the silent treatment is to refuse any form of verbal communication with them. It is used as a form of manipulative punishment.

"I will not allow anyone to walk in my mind with dirty feet."

-Gandhi

Chapter 14:

Overcoming the meta blockers

———

——

—

call any entity that impairs one's meta intelligence a *meta blocker*. A meta blocker can be physiological, psychological, or sociological. Removing meta blockers can be difficult because, ironically, they are blocking your awareness of them.

PHYSIOLOGICAL

———

—

Examples of physiological meta blockers are…

- alcohol addiction
- drug addiction
- poor diet / exercise regimen
- lack of sleep
- stress

You must obviously take measures to remove them from your life as soon as possible.

———

—

A common example of a sociological meta blocker is friends who are a negative influence. The best thing you can do for yourself is find new friends. As renowned motivational speaker, Jim Rohn, famously observed …

*"You are the average of the five
people you spend the most time with."*

-Jim Rohn

Choose your friends wisely, for they largely influence the path you will take in life.

"Show me your friends and I will show you your future."

-anonymous sage

PSYCHOLOGICAL

———

—

Psychological meta blockers are interesting because they can be harder to identify. Often, the individual is high functioning, so the blockers are masked by other traits that are more appealing.

Throughout college and my career, I've met very intelligent people who were not able to grow because they were afflicted with one meta blocker or another. I have categorized them into the following psychological archetypes…

THE EGOTIST

One of the biggest blockers I observed was ego. As a matter of fact, it is more like a constellation of blockers revolving around the ego center. An over-inflated ego gives rise to a slew of other blockers such as:

- overconfidence
- not acknowledging weaknesses
- not acknowledging mistakes

- always having to be right / can't be wrong
- know-it-all-ism

*"A know-it-all is a person who knows everything
except for how annoying he is."*

-Demetri Martin

*

Thinking you know everything prevents you from learning anything

*

*"Throw out your conceited opinions, for it is impossible for a
person to learn what he thinks he already knows."*

- Epictetus

THE NARCISSIST

A narcissist is essentially an egotist on steroids. In addition to possessing all the traits of an egotist, a narcissist is also characterized by blockers such as:

- Vanity

Vanity clouds your judgement.

*"Vanity working on a weak head
produces every sort of mischief."*

-Jane Austen

Narcissists think that everybody adores them, but the opposite is true.

*"Do you wish people to speak well of you?
Don't speak well of yourself."*

-Blaise Pascal

- Sense of entitlement

It is important to realize that nobody owes you anything. If you want something, you have to work for it just like everybody else.

- Not accepting of criticism

- Lack of empathy

People who lack empathy cannot understand others.
If we cannot understand others, we cannot really understand ourselves.

THE SELF-SABOTEUR

At the opposite end from the superiority (ego) complex, we have the inferiority complex which gives rise to such blockers as…

- self-doubt
- self-limiting beliefs
- negative attitudes
- negative thinking
- negative self-talk

Self-limiting beliefs are like an anchor that won't let you set sail. Remove the anchor and you will discover a whole new world.

*

The only limits you have are the ones you set for yourself, because after all, it is your beliefs that create your reality.

*

THE NEUROTIC

Neurotics spend all their time worrying hence they have no time for self-reflection and improvement. Constant worrying leads to chronic stress and anxiety which impair one's judgement and reasoning. It is said that the coward dies a thousand deaths. This is true also of the worrier. Most of the things we worry about will never come to pass…

"We suffer more in our imagination than in reality."
-Seneca

The remainder are very trivial…

*"If you want to test your memory, try to recall
what you were worrying about one year today."*

-E. J. Cossman

THE VICTIM

People with a victim complex seek persecution because this gets them attention and allows them to avoid responsibility. Their locus of control is entirely external, and they typically suffer from learned helplessness and hopelessness. They are also quick to blame others for their miserable state. They believe life is unfair and everybody's out to get them. Needless to say, the victim mindset is not conducive to personal growth.

> *"Playing the victim card blinds you to your own flaws and so you can never improve. Self-pity is the easiest way to create unilateral misery."*
>
> *-Sri Sri*

THE DREAMER

> *"I never dreamt of success. I worked for it."*
>
> *-Estee Lauder*

Sometimes people will recognize they have a negative attitude and try to become more positive - which is good, except that they over-compensate and develop what I call the *dreamer complex.* The dreamer complex is characterized by …

- 'pipe dreaming'
- unrealistic thinking
- laziness (physical & mental)

*

Don't wish for things to happen; make them happen.

*

Dreamers don't plan or take action towards their goals. Instead they wait for someone or something to show them the way - they usually wind up waiting an awfully long time. They shouldn't expect a harvest when they haven't tended the land.

"A goal without a plan is just a wish"

-Antoine de Saint Exupery

THE BIGOT

Another pervasive meta blocker is bigotry. Bigotry is marked by ...

- Intolerance towards those who hold different opinions
- closed-mindedness
- intellectual stubbornness

It goes without saying that these traits are not conducive to intellectual growth.

THE FATALIST

The final group of psychological meta blockers I wish to discuss falls under the fatalism complex. This is when people are convinced that their lot in life is pre-determined and there is nothing that they can do to change it. This is an extremely debilitating *disease* and there might be several reasons for it. People may have been programmed to think this way by their parents or their teachers or they may hold superstitious or irrational beliefs. Another culprit is the IQ myth which so many people accept as gospel.

Carol Dweck has written extensively about the *growth mindset* and its unfortunate opposite: the *fixed mindset* (Dweck, 2006). Some people have a growth mindset and some a fixed mindset. Those with a fixed mindset believe that their intellectual capacity is capped by their genes and can't be improved while those with the growth mindset have no such limiting belief and continue to grow intellectually.

Those with a fixed mindset believe they are immutably smart or dumb. Those who believe they are dumb will avoid challenges because they view their efforts as futile. But the interesting thing is that those who view themselves as smart will also avoid challenges because they tie their identity to success at doing things - failing at the challenge would 'prove' they are dumb. Those with a growth mindset, however, embrace challenges as an opportunity to learn and grow.

It is absolutely astonishing how one simple belief can have such a tremendous impact on one's life. Dweck writes…

For twenty years, my research has shown that the view you adopt for yourself profoundly affects the way you lead your life. It can determine whether you become the person you want to be and whether you accomplish the things you value.

Fortunately, Dweck also found that fixed mindset children who were taught the growth mindset quickly adopted that new mindset and flourished with it.

"Our first fundamental problem for development is fatalism. People do not believe they can influence their future."

-Mwalimu Musheshe

Chapter 15:

The Meta Intelligentsia

———
——
—

The uber successful individuals I highlight in this chapter are examples of people with great meta intelligence. I call them *the meta intelligentsia.* Primarily, they have SMARTER thinking skills and bigger SHARKS than most. We can all learn a lot by studying the way they think.

Jeff Bezos

Founder and CEO of ecommerce giant Amazon, Bezos' net worth of $150B makes him the richest man in history. Bezos also founded aero space company, Blue Origin in 2000.

MQualities:

Innovative and adaptive thinker. Bezos likes to experiment. Uses mental models: regret minimization, root cause analysis, second order thinking.

MQuotes:

"I always had a passion for invention."

"I was always thinking of how to improve things."

"You must proceed adaptively."

Bill Gates

Bill Gates cofounded the world's largest software business, Microsoft, and subsequently became the richest man in the world until he was superseded by Jeff Bezos.

MQualities:

Bill is a voracious reader and a systems, computational, & adaptive thinker.

MQuotes:

"Success is a lousy teacher. It seduces smart people into thinking they can't lose."

"If you are born poor it's not your mistake, but if you die poor it's your mistake."

"Treatment without prevention is simply unsustainable."

Warren Buffett

The 'oracle of Omaha' is arguably the most successful investor of all time. As head of his investment company, Berkshire Hathaway, Buffett became one of the richest men in the world.

MQualities:

Buffet is a voracious reader and uses mental models such as circle of competence.

MQuotes:

"The most important investment you can make is in yourself."

"I just sit in my office and read all day."

"I insist on a lot of time being spent, almost every day, to just sit and think."

Charlie Munger

Charlie Munger is vice-chairman of Berkshire Hathaway. Together with Warren Buffet, they grew the company into the investment behemoth that it is now. Munger is also famous for popularizing mental models in his speeches and in his book, *Poor Charlie's Almanac*.

MQualities:

Charlie is a multidisciplinary autodidact. He is a systems thinker and uses perspective-switching. He uses numerous mental models such as inversion.

MQuotes:

"Spend each day trying to be a little wiser than you were when you woke up."

"If you skillfully follow the multidisciplinary path, you will never wish to come back. It would be like cutting off your hands."

"I paid no attention to the territorial boundaries of academic disciplines and I just grabbed all the big ideas that I could."

Mark Zuckerberg

Mark Zuckerberg was a programming prodigy who at the age of 12 created a messaging app called ZuckNet that would be a precursor of things to come. While at Harvard,

Zuckerberg began to create the social media app, Facebook. Facebook would go on to have billions of users and make Zuckerberg billions of dollars! In 2010, Vanity Fair named Zuckerberg the most influential person of the information age!

MQualities:

Zuckerberg is a risk taker, persistent, and an adaptive thinker.

MQuotes:

"Sometimes we are going to do stuff that's controversial, and we're going to make mistakes. We have to be willing to take risks."

"It's ok to break things to make them better."

"The thing that we are trying to do at Facebook, is just help people connect and communicate more efficiently."

Elon Musk

The multi-faceted Musk has launched companies in remarkably diverse industries such as PayPal, SpaceX, Tesla Motors. Musk has always had a huge thirst for knowledge and an entrepreneurial spirit. As a youngster, Musk would read two books a day, and he taught himself programming and sold his first computer program at age 12.

MQualities:

Musk is an autodidact polymath on steroids! He is persistent and resilient as well as a task-conscious and systems / computational thinker.

He uses mental models such as first order principles.

MQuotes:

"People work better when they know what the goal is and why. It is important that people look forward to coming to work in the morning and enjoy working."

"When something is important enough, you do it even if the odds are not in your favor."

"When I was in college, I wanted to be involved in things that would change the world."

Richard Branson

Richard Branson launched Virgin Records in the early 1970s, eventually building his business into the diverse multinationa Virgin Group.

MQualities:

Branson is an independent thinker, resilient, curious, & creative.

MQuotes:

"Do not be embarrassed by your failures, learn from them and start again."

"A business has to be involving, it has to be fun, and it has to exercise your creative instincts."

"One thing is certain in business. You and everyone around you will make mistakes."

Mark Cuban

Celebrity entrepreneur and investor, Mark Cuban is a star on the hit reality show, Shark Tank where budding entrepreneurs pitch their products to moguls like Cuban. Mark is an avid sports fan and owner of the NBA's Dallas Mavericks. He is also a movie buff and owns Magnolia Pictures. The charismatic Cuban has appeared in numerous cameo roles on the silver screen and tv.

MQualities:

Mark is an independent thinker, constant learner, & resilient.

MQuotes:

"Love what you do or don't do it."

"What I've learned … is you just got to stay focused and believe in yourself and trust your own ability and judgment."

"I'm continuously looking for ways to improve all my companies"

Tony Robbins

The most famous life coach on the planet has millions of followers. He has worked with U.S. presidents as well as top athletes and entertainers. He also happens to run a multi-billion-dollar business empire.

MQualities:

Tony is a Kaizen devotee, metacognitive thinker and adept at social meta skills such as cognitive empathy, perspective-switching, persuasion, & perception.

MQuotes:

"If you keep doing what you've always done, you'll keep getting what you've always gotten."

"We're drowning in information but starving for wisdom."

"Success without fulfillment is the ultimate failure."

Steve Jobs

Steve Jobs is yet another college dropout who went on to build a mega successful company – in his case, the most valuable company in the world, Apple Computer.

At Apple, the ever-innovative Jobs designed products such as the iPod, iPad, & iPhone which revolutionized the way we communicate, learn, & entertain ourselves.

MQualities:

The late great tech visionary was an innovative and independent thinker. He always had one eye on the big picture and the other eye on the details.

MQuotes:

The following quote of Jobs' is one of my favourites and it could just as easily describe the meta intelligentsia…

"Here's to the crazy ones. The misfits. The rebels. The troublemakers. The round pegs in the square holes. The ones who see things differently. They're not fond of rules. And they have no respect for the status quo. You can quote them, disagree with them, glorify or vilify them. About the only thing you can't do is ignore them. Because they change things. They push the human race forward. And while some may see them as the crazy ones, we see genius. Because the people who are crazy enough to think they can change the world, are the ones who do."

And just for good measure, I've included a couple of outstanding successful meta intelligent individuals from the past…

Thomas Edison

Thomas Edison is arguably the greatest inventor of all time. He is famous of course for inventing the first practical incandescent light bulb, but he also held patents for over 1000 inventions including the phonograph and movie camera.

MQualities:

Edison was curious, creative, inventive, persistent, and a constant learner.

He was a resourceful and task-conscious thinker. Edison liked to use the incubation technique to allow his subconscious to work on problems overnight.

MQuotes:

"Genius is 1% inspiration and 99% perspiration."

"I have not failed. I've just found 10,000 ways that won't work."

"There's a way to do it better - find it."

Benjamin Franklin

Ben Franklin was a man of many talents. He was an accomplished inventor, scientist, politician, writer, and publisher. He is well-known as one of the founding fathers of the United States and for inventing bifocal glasses.

MQualities:

Franklin was the quintessential autodidact polymath. He was inventive and a resourceful thinker.

MQuotes:

Franklin published Poor Richard's Almanac which contained many of his witty aphorisms…

"Lost time is never found again."

"An investment in knowledge always pays the best interest."

"He that lies down with dogs, shall rise up with fleas."

CHAPTER 16:

EPILOGUE

ociety is becoming increasingly more complex. We are more connected than ever with others, albeit digitally, not physically. Thanks to the internet, we have more access to information than ever before. IQ and EQ will no longer be sufficient to manage this newfound complexity. We need a different way of dealing with people and knowledge - meta intelligence is that way.

After reading this book, you will begin to think more meta intelligently. Both your self-awareness and social awareness will improve. You will begin to cultivate meta intelligent skills, habits, attitudes, resources, & knowledge, and begin to see things in new ways that others cannot.

While I am confident this book will help you to achieve success and attain the things you've always desired, my main hope is that this book will help you to improve yourself as well as help you improve our world.

"You cannot hope to build a better world without improving the individuals. To that end, each of us must work for our own improvement."

- Marie Curie

APPENDIX 1:

ARE YOU META INTELLIGENT?

———

——

—

To find out just how meta intelligent you are, take the following MQ test. It is a comprehensive assessment tool consisting of 100 statements that cover all aspects of meta intelligence. Simply answer yes if you agree with the statement or no if you disagree. Record your responses.

The Meta Intelligence Test

———

—

1. I believe other factors are more important than IQ for achieving success.
2. I am very resourceful.
3. I like to think about my thoughts.
4. I am good at clearing my mind of negative thoughts.
5. I am always evaluating things and processes with the aim of improving them.
6. Awareness of one's thoughts is essential for self-mastery.
7. I actively manage / update my skill set.
8. I am aware of my strengths and weaknesses.
9. I like to think of new ways of doing things.
10. I am good at evaluating.

11. I evaluate the strategies I use to learn.
12. Learning should be a lifelong habit.
13. I think critically.
14. I am good at recognizing patterns.
15. I like to analyze things.
16. I am good at abstracting the important features from information.
17. I am not very superstitious.
18. I rarely jump to conclusions.
19. I see most things as being shades of grey rather than black and white.
20. I like to set goals.

21. Overall, I am pleased with the outcomes of my decisions.
22. I am good at adapting to changing circumstances.
23. Time is a precious resource - I manage it wisely.
24. I enjoy thinking *outside the box*.
25. I set daily priorities.
26. I constantly try to improve myself.
27. I regularly review my goals.
28. I like to read self-improvement books.
29. I like to ask myself insightful questions.
30. I regularly engage in self-reflection.

31. I regularly write down my thoughts in a journal.
32. I have a morning ritual.
33. I write down my ideas.
34. I enjoy playing strategy games or doing puzzles.
35. I take care of my mind and body.
36. I focus on the important tasks.
37. I don't dwell on the past.
38. I have a positive attitude.
39. I have an open mind.

40. I am very flexible.
41. I check my ego at the door.
42. I am not afraid to stand out from the crowd.
43. I am not afraid to step out of my comfort zone.
44. I am not anxious about the future because I am confidant I can adapt to any change or solve any problem.
45. I don't wish for things to happen; I make them happen.
46. My locus of control is internal.
47. I have a can-do attitude.
48. I believe in constant & never-ending improvement.
49. I am persistent in achieving my objectives.
50. I am not afraid of failure.

51. I learn from my mistakes and move on.

52. I like challenges.
53. My attitude can overcome any hardship or obstacle.
54. I am resilient in the face of setbacks.
55. I have a wide-spread curiosity.
56. I like being creative.
57. I consider myself to be an objective person.
58. I associate with success-minded people.
59. I make good use of technology.
60. I try to come up with many solutions to a problem.

61. I evaluate how I think.
62. I try to optimize the way I do things whenever I can.
63. I am aware of what I know and don't know.
64. What I know is small compared to what I don't know.
65. I acknowledge my shortcomings.
66. I am receptive to constructive criticism.
67. I believe there is no limit to what I can accomplish.
68. I nip negative self-talk in the bud.
69. I don't spend time worrying.
70. Knowing what you want is not enough; you need to plan as well.

71. Knowing what you want is not enough; you need to take action as well.
72. I objectively evaluate the merits of opinions that are contrary to mine.
73. It is important to notice what's working and what's not working.
74. My intellectual capacity is not fixed.
75. I read every day.
76. I don't mind admitting I don't know something.
77. I don't mind admitting when I'm wrong.
78. I am aware of my biases.
79. I calculate the consequences of my actions.
80. I observe the effect my actions have on others.

81. I choose my friends carefully.
82. I cut loose negative people.
83. I try to determine what other people are thinking.
84. I know when someone is trying to manipulate me.
85. I try to ascertain the motives behind a person's actions.
86. I try to gage how others see me.
87. I try to predict people's behaviour.
88. I seek good role models &/or mentors.
89. I like to observe how skilled / successful people do things.
90. I try to anticipate how people will react to my actions.

91. I seek feedback from others.
92. I am not afraid to ask people for help.
93. I always try to learn something from others.
94. I try to determine others' strengths and weaknesses.
95. I am curious as to why people do the things they do.
96. I avoid toxic people.
97. I don't enter into dysfunctional relationships.
98. I don't fall for scams.
99. I am a good lie detector.
100.   I can recognize when people are playing mind games.

HOW DID YOU FARE?

———

—

Your number of yes answers indicate the degree to which you think and act like a meta intelligent person.

If you scored low, do not despair, for unlike IQ, you can improve your MQ score by increasing your awareness and understanding of areas where you did not do so well.

Appendix 2: Meta Mental Models

"Give me a lever long enough and a fulcrum on which to place it, and I shall move the world."

-Archimedes

Mental models are cognitive tools that help explain reality. In this section I list 10 high leverage mental models that can be universally applied across many disciplines and situations.

1. The map is not the territory
2. Abstraction
3. Pareto Principle
4. Divide and Conquer
5. Working Backwards
6. The Horizon Effect
7. Dirty Dishes
8. Ideological Bubbles
9. Going on *Tilt*
10. Dickens Process

The map is not the Territory

It is appropriate to begin with this mental model because it reminds us that any model, whether a map or mental model, is not the actual thing being modeled; however, if skillfully constructed, it can be very useful while if not carefully constructed, it can be very dangerous (e.g. stock market models). Models approximate reality, thus, the mental models we use should be continuously refined based on feedback.

Abstraction

A map or model is an example of an abstraction. Abstraction is the process of removing the unessential details from something in order to remain with only the important and pertinent features. Abstraction is vital because our world is so complex. We need abstraction in order to understand and deal with all the complicated systems and subsystems of life.

We also need abstraction in order to prevent being overwhelmed with information. We abstract only the most applicable information and discard the rest.

Pareto Principle

> *"My success, part of it certainly, is that I have focused in on a few things."*
>
> -Bill Gates

Pareto's Principle (a.k.a. 80/20 rule) is probably the most often cited mental model and it is indeed one of the most useful to know. It was named after Vilfredo Pareto, a 19th century Italian economist, who noticed that 80% of the land in Italy was owned by 20% of the population.

It turns out that this type of asymmetrical relationship occurs in many areas of life where a minority of inputs are responsible for a majority of the output. With respect to tasks, a minority of your tasks will account for the majority of your results, so it pays to identify and prioritize those more valuable tasks (the 20%).

And knowing what <u>not</u> to prioritize (i.e. the 80%) is equally important as Steve Jobs makes clear in this passage:

> "People think focus means saying yes to the thing you've got to focus on. But that's not what it means at all. It means saying no to the hundred other good ideas that there are. You have to pick carefully. I'm actually as proud of the things we haven't done as the things we have done."

Divide and Conquer

This is a great mental model for solving complex problems. Divide and conquer works by recursively breaking down a problem into two or more sub-problems until these become simple enough to be solved directly. The solutions to the sub-problems are combined to give a solution to the original problem.

It is also a useful mental model for breaking down complex tasks into smaller more manageable components.

Working Backwards

Traditional problem-solving proceeds from an initial state (problem) to an end state (solution). The working backwards approach takes the reverse route, one works backwards from the goal or desired end state to the current state. This is useful when the solution involves many steps or intermediate solutions.

A goal may also be viewed as an nth order effect of a cause and effect chain. We find the immediate cause of the goal (which is the last step) and that then becomes the n-1 effect and we work backwards through the chain in this manner until we reach the initial cause.

Working backwards is one of the many mental models Jeff Bezos uses at Amazon. Their approach is to work backwards from the satisfied customer!

The Horizon Effect

A lot of the problems we face as a society today are the direct result of what I refer to as the *horizon effect*. The horizon effect is an old computer chess term from the early days of computer chess.

The first chess computers could see only a couple of moves ahead; if they could capture your queen on their move, they would do so, even if it meant they would be checkmated on the next move. These primitive chess programs were said to suffer from a horizon effect where everything looked rosy until they got checkmated. Checkmate was beyond their horizon.

Many people today are like those early chess programs; they can only see one move ahead, and so they cannot see beyond the horizon of their superficial actions. Meta intelligent people on the other hand can see many moves ahead. They are second order thinkers that can calculate the long-term consequences of an action.

The good news is that second order thinking is a skill that can be developed with practice, much like chess players can improve their vision with practice.

"Failing to consider second- and third-order consequences is the cause of a lot of painfully bad decisions, and it is especially deadly when the first inferior option confirms your own biases. Never seize on the first available option, no matter how good it seems, before you've asked questions and explored."

-Ray Dalio

Dirty Dishes

This model comes to us curtesy of, film icon, Arnold Schwarzenegger! The *Terminator* star likes to use dirty dishes in the sink as a metaphor for how important it is to tackle unsavory or difficult tasks right away, otherwise they will only get harder – much like crud on dishes hardens with time, making them more difficult to clean later on.

Ideological Bubbles

An ideological bubble (a.k.a. information bubble or echo chamber) is the situation that occurs when an individual becomes insulated from counter ideologies or viewpoints (often political e.g. conservative vs liberal).

One cause for this bubble may be that the individual surrounds themselves solely with like-minded people. One should seek open social networks (diverse viewpoints) vs closed networks (homogenized viewpoints).

Another reason may be that their information comes solely from news sources that espouse their views. News organizations have become increasingly divided along partisan political lines, so it is advisable to get your news from a variety of sources.

Filter bubbles

One type of ideological bubble that has grown in importance in tandem with the rise of sophisticated internet search engines and social media is the filter bubble. The term was coined by internet activist, Eli Pariser, who realized that 'personalized' search algorithms such as Google's that guess what information a user would like to see based on information about the user's past click-behaviour and search history inevitably isolate users in their own ideological bubbles. (Pariser, 2011)

Social media algorithms such as Facebook's behave in a similar fashion with the result that the user is under the illusion that most people think the same way they do.

Going on *Tilt*

This is a poker term that in turn was borrowed from pinball players who would tilt the pinball machine when they were frustrated that the ball wasn't bouncing their way (which resulted in the paddles locking). When a poker player suffers a 'bad beat' there is a strong tendency to get frustrated and let their emotions get the best of them. Still fixated on the big loss of the previous hand, they lose their concentration and begin to make unsound decisions the rest of game. They are said to have gone on tilt. Avoiding going on tilt and recognizing when others are on tilt is an important component of being a good poker player.

Going on tilt is a useful mental model to know even if you are not a pinball player or a poker player. There are many times in life when the ball just doesn't bounce your way or someone else gets dealt a better hand. You must remember to keep your cool and not let your judgement be affected. Unfortunately, people go on tilt all the time, such as after losing money on a stock or when a rival gets the coveted promotion.

"In every discipline, the ability to be clearheaded, present, cool under fire is much of what separates the best from the mediocre."

-Josh Waitzkin

The Dickens Process

This mental model is named after Charles Dickens, who wrote *A Christmas Carol*. One of the characters in the story, Scrooge, is a selfish miser until he is visited by the ghost of Christmas future who shows Scrooge how miserable he will be if he doesn't change and become a kinder, more generous person.

To use this technique, you typically envision two paths for yourself: one path maintains the bad habit or feature about yourself; the other is the path without the negative characteristic. You visualize and actively feel how life will be like at different stages down the different roads e.g. after 1,5,

& 10 years. This process has been used with great success by Tony Robbins at his seminars. Participants can visualize the long-term consequences of not changing and so will readily change.

The process can also be modified to be a decision tool where you visualize the long-term effects of two different choices.

Post Scriptum:

Pandemic Lessons

"An ounce of prevention is worth a pound of cure."

-Benjamin Franklin

As I get ready to publish this book, the world is paralyzed amid a pandemic, and before publishing I feel compelled to offer some thoughts on this tragedy that has affected so many lives.

The toll of the pandemic, in terms of both lives and jobs lost, is unimaginable. In fact, many have called this a *black swan* event: devastating but unpredictable. Nevertheless, the truth of the matter is that for one segment of the population at least, it wasn't unpredictable: meta intelligent individuals knew a pandemic was coming. It wasn't a matter of if but when. Bill Gates had been sounding the alarm for years. Economic and health experts had been imploring governments to prepare for a pandemic ever since the SARS outbreak in 2003. Tragically, their pleas went unheeded.

Alas, governments didn't learn anything from the SARS outbreak. Instead of wildlife markets being banned, they flourished. Instead of hospitals and health departments being equipped to deal with the *next one*, their budgets were slashed. The level of incompetence on a global scale is truly astounding. I don't think we have ever witnessed such a colossal failure across all governments. I apologize for venting my frustration, but it is hard to remain stoic when people close to you are suffering. I try to be rational, but I am not a machine.

Not being able to see danger is the first failure of an adaptive system. But what about once the danger is upon us? Here again there was practically universal failure.

Alarm bells were ringing all throughout the unfolding catastrophe. Governments had many opportunities to implement prophylactic measures at various stages of the outbreak but didn't, e.g., when it was first learned that:

- an extremely infectious SARS-like novel coronavirus was spreading throughout China
(A novel virus is a new virus that humans haven't been exposed to before, thus they have no immunity to it and there is no vaccine immediately available. If the initial cases are not contained, it will spread rapidly throughout a population.)

- There were thousands of flights still going in and out of China.

- a significant proportion of carriers were asymptomatic and were shedding the virus.
This was a game changer that was met with little more than a collective shrug despite the fact it would make the tracking and isolating of carriers extremely difficult. Authorities still relied on self-reporting and voluntary self-isolation by symptomatic carriers as opposed to more widespread diagnostic testing and mandatory quarantining.

This was all known by the end of January, and yet in the ensuing month, governments still inexplicably did little or nothing to mitigate the disaster. E.g. widespread testing was not available, and there were shortages of ventilators and personal protective equipment (PPE).

But even if your government was unprepared, that didn't mean you had to be caught off guard. News travels fast in today's world and China's epidemic was making headlines throughout the globe. The meta intelligent began prepping for self-isolation long before social distancing officially kicked in.

But what about everyone else? How can we account for why so many people were caught flat-footed?

———

—

Let's examine some of the common cognitive mistakes that were made. If you fell victim to any of them, you can use it as a lesson to prepare for the next disruptive event.

THINKING ERRORS

Not thinking adaptively

The pandemic demonstrated how important good situational awareness (SA) skills are. Unfortunately, it also demonstrated that many people are lacking in these skills. But they can be learned, and the pandemic serves as an instructive case study.

If you recall, there are three phases of SA: (1) Perception, (2) Comprehension, & (3) Projection. There were failures at each of these stages:

1. People were not attuned to changes happening in the world. People were not able to filter out disinformation

from governments and news sources. (see abstraction & filter bubbles below)
2. If people did manage to obtain the correct information, they did not analyze and evaluate it properly. (see biases and mental models below)
3. Some people were able to comprehend the situation, but they were not able to accurately predict the trajectory the virus would take in terms of both space and time.

The consequence of these missteps is that people (and governments) were not able to take corrective action quickly enough.

Not thinking in terms of systems / second order thinking

The world we live in is a grand eco system where nations are now more interconnected than ever before. Something that happens in one part of the globe will inevitably affect other parts of the globe. When an elephant like China sneezes, other nations are likely to catch a cold.

"Realize that everything connects to everything else"

-Leonardo Da Vinci

Not evolving one's thinking

It is apparent that many people are not knowledgeable about viruses or how our immune system works. Mistaken beliefs abound such as people thinking that as long as they don't eat bats, they're safe, or that taking antibiotics will kill the virus.

One should be proactively autodidactic and learn about how biosystems work. Bill Gates is not a virologist, but he is practically an expert in the field because he spent a lot of time learning about it.

Not thinking rationally

- People were indulging in risky behaviour: refusing to social distance, shaking hands, partying, etc.
- Some people believed the virus would magically disappear (magical thinking)
- It is clear, judging from all the kooky cures and conspiracy theories that were promulgated, that many people are not inclined to think scientifically. They need to be more evidence-based thinkers.

BIASED THINKING

Visibility Bias

*

People can't wrap their heads around something they can't see.

*

Optimism Bias

> *"Don't worry about a thing 'cause
> every little thing gonna be alright."*
>
> -Bob Marley

This is thinking that everything will turn out all right without any justification. People with an optimism bias are convinced that the virus will somehow spare them. It is good not to obsessively worry about something, but one must also be prepared.

> *"Hope for the best but prepare for the worst."*
>
> -popular adage

Invincibility Bias

People with an invincibility bias are not afraid of catching the virus because they think that they can easily beat it. Many people think that nothing can harm them; that they are invincible. They usually find out the hard way that they are not.

Ethnocentric Bias

This is the tendency to believe that other cultures / societies are inferior to yours. Thus, other countries may not be able to manage an epidemic, but one's own undoubtedly will.

Confirmation Bias

People dismissed information they disagreed with.

MENTAL MODELS

Not being aware of mental models or failing to implement them properly can also lead to biased or faulty thinking.

e.g.

Exponential Growth

Thinking linearly and not grasping the speed of exponential growth.

Suppose something doubles every day so that at the end of the first day there will be two cases and at the end of 3, 8 cases. Now things start to take off so that at the end of one week there will be 128 cases and at the end of two weeks there will be 16,384 cases. After 5 more days there will be half a million cases! That's the power of exponential growth.

A novel virus like the covid-19 virus will spread exponentially until people take prophylactic measures or they acquire immunity.

Abstraction

People were overwhelmed by noise e.g. distractions, disinformation, & misinformation. They missed the signal i.e. important and accurate information. It is important to seek out credible news sources and to filter your texts and emails as well.

Filter Bubbles

Customized internet search engine algorithms that guess what information a user would like to see based on their personal information inevitably isolate users in their own ideological filter bubbles.

Social media platforms like Facebook have similar algorithms with the result that their news feeds expose the user primarily to sources who share their point of view.

If the political party you are affiliated with is in power, then your news sources will likely be supportive of the government, while if the opposition party is in power, then your news sources will likely be critical of the government.

It is important to be conscious of this fact and to actively seek out alternative viewpoints.

Cognitive Empathy

Not taking the perspective of governments into account and realizing that they may be disinclined to disclose embarrassing information.

Not taking the perspective of big business into account and realizing that it may not be in their financial interests to advocate social distancing.

HOW WE CAN ADAPT TO THE PANDEMIC

———

—

Welcome to the new reality. The way of life we knew, before the pandemic, has been upended. Undoubtedly, some sectors will suffer, and many businesses will close; however, others will rise in their place and new opportunities will crop up.

The key is not to panic and approach the situation calmly. Maintain a positive attitude and think resourcefully of ways you can advantageously adapt to the new conditions.

One adaptation technique is to identify and examine the changes brought on by a disruptive event and see if there are any new niches created where one can move into. So, let's look at some second order effects of the pandemic. The following is a sample of those domains likely to grow:

1. Telework
2. Home office equipment
3. Virtual meeting tools (e.g. zoom, skype)
4. Automation e.g. in factories & warehouses; self-driving vehicles
5. Automation tools

6. Automation engineers
7. Virology / vaccinology
8. Epidemiology / immunology
9. Personal protective equipment (e.g. gloves, masks)
10. Medical equipment (e.g. ventilators)
11. Drive-through & take-out restaurants vs dine-in
12. Cooking appliances (e.g. bread makers)
13. Online shopping
14. Delivery companies
15. Online education
16. Online coaching / masterminds
17. Virtual health care
18. Virtual entertainment
19. Virtual gyms
20. Home gym equipment
21. Video games / board games
22. Books / e-books

Once we have identified areas for growth, we can then proceed to advantageously position ourselves in those segments of the economy.

Another adaptation technique I propose is to implement the SHARK system for the brave new world we find ourselves in. Review the SHARK elements in this book and highlight the ones which will be especially useful; then determine and write down any new elements you will need (as dictated by your personal circumstances).

e.g.

Skills:

Computational thinking

SMARTER thinking and learning

Adaptability

Habits:

Self-education

Attitudes:

Positive thinking

Resilience (avoid going on tilt)

Flexibility

Resources:

Coaches, masterminds

Internet, online courses

Knowledge:

Biomedical: e.g. virology, epidemiology

Psychology: e.g. stress management, cognitive distortions, biases, mental models

Technology: e.g. software engineering, web design

E-Careers: e.g. blogger, vlogger, coach, instructor, marketer, writer (ebooks, articles)

=-=-=

I hope this section, and indeed this book, has been helpful in providing you with inspiration and some useful ideas on how to best navigate the new landscape.

Take care,

Justice

BIBLIOGRAPHY

Adams, S. (2013). *How to Fail at Almost Everything and Still Win Big.*

Anderson, L. W., Krathwohl, D. R., & others. (2001). *A Taxonomy for Learning, Teaching, and Assessing.*

Aurelius, M. (n.d.). *Meditations.*

Barrett, D. (2001). *The Committee of Sleep: How artists, scientists, and athletes use their dreams for creative problem solving...*

Bolton, R. (1979). *People Skills.*

Bradberry, T. (2015). Why Your Boss Lacks Emotional Intelligence. *Forbes.*

Bradberry, T., & Greaves, J. (2009). *Emotional Intelligence 2.0.*

Carnegie, D. (1936). *How to Win Friends and Influence People.*

Charney, C. (2003). *The Portable Mentor.*

Corley, T. (2009). *Rich Habits.*

Covey, S. R. (1989). *The 7 Habits of Highly Effective People.*

Dalio, R. (2017). *Principles.*

De Bono, E. (2014). *Lateral Thinking: An Introduction.*

Dobelli, R. (2013). *The Art of Thinking Clearly.*

Duncker, K. (1945). On Problem Solving. *Psychological Monographs.*

Dweck, C. (2006). *Mindset: The New Psychology of Success.*

Endsley, M. (1995). Toward a theory of situational awareness in dynamic systems. *Human Factors.*

Epictetus. (n.d.). *A Manual for Living.*

Ericsson, A., & Pool, R. (2016). *Peak: Secrets from the new science of expertise.*

Erlandson, D. (2012). *How To Think Clearly: A guide to critical thinking.*

Ferriss, T. (2011). *The 4-Hour Work Week.*

Ferriss, T. (2016). *Tools of Titans.*

Ferriss, T. (2017). *Tribe of Mentors.*

Gardner, H. (1983). *Frames of Mind: The theory of multiple intelligences.*

Gardner, J. W. (1964). *Self-Renewal: The individual and the innovative society.*

Gladwell, M. (2008). *Outliers: The story of success.*

Hadfield, C. (2013). *An Astronaut's Guide to Life on Earth.*

Hill, N. (1928). *Law of Success.*

Hill, N. (1937). *Think and Grow Rich.*

Kahneman, D. (2011). *Thinking Fast and Thinking Slow.*

Kamin, L. J. (1974). *The Science and Politics of I.Q.*

Machiavelli, N. (n.d.). *The Prince.*

Maxwell, J. C. (2007). *Failing Forward: Turning mistakes into stepping stones for success*

Maxwell, J. C. (2011). *The Power of Winning: Motivation and inspiration on how to be a winner.*

Maxwell, J. C. (2014). *The 15 Invaluable Laws of Growth.*

Munger, C. T. (2005). *Poor Charlie's Almanac: The wit and wisdom of Charles T. Munger.*

Osborn, A. F. (1953). *Applied Imagination.*

Pariser, E. (2011). *The Filter Bubble: How the new personalized web is changing what we read and how we think.*

Robbins, T. (1986). *Ultimate Power.*

Robbins, T. (1991). *Awaken the Giant Within.*

Roige, A. (2014, April 29). *Intelligence and IQ testing.* Retrieved from eugenicsarchive.ca:
http://eugenicsarchive.ca/discover/tree/535eecb77095aa000000023a

Seabrook, R., & Dienes, Z. (2003). *Incubation in Problem Solving as a Context Effect.*

Seneca. (n.d.). *Letters from a Stoic.*

Seneca. (n.d.). *On the Shortness of Life.*

Senge, P. M. (2010). *The Fifth Discipline: The art and practice of the learning organization.*

Sivers, D. (2011). *Anything You Want: 40 lessons for a new kind of entrepreneur.*

Stanovich, K. (2015). Rational and Irrational Thought: The thinking that IQ tests miss. *Scientific American.*

Stone, W. C. (1962). *The Success System That Never Fails.*

Swanson, H. L. (1990). Influence of metacognitive knowledge and aptitude on problem solving. *Journal of Educational Psychology.*

Taleb, N. (2007). *The Black Swan: The impact of the highly improbable.*

Taleb, N. (2012). *Antifragile: Things that gain from disorder.*

Tzu, L. (n.d.). *Tao Te Ching.*

Tzu, S. (n.d.). *The Art of War.*

Waitzkin, J. (2007). *The Art of Learning: An inner journey to optimal performance.*

Weinberg, G., & McCann, L. (2019). *Super Thinking: The big book of mental models.*

9 798642 543443